TO FAY
heroine of this book

Contents

Preface to the New Edition

*T*HIS volume was first written to celebrate the nation's bicentennial as one of a series to include all fifty states. Sponsorship was by the American Association for State and Local History, funding by the National Endowment for the Humanities, and publication by W. W. Norton & Company. This is the first appearance of the Arizona volume in paperback format.

It is fitting that it come from the university press of Arizona's sister state. New Mexico and Arizona began as remote outposts of New Spain, then Mexico, and were finally seized by conquest from Mexico and made the single United States Territory of New Mexico. They entered the union a month apart in 1912 as the forty-seventh and forty-eighth states.

In tracing these often violent changes in an arid land, first held by Indian tribes, it can be seen that its evolution was affected by the land itself, its mountains, rivers, and deserts. It also became clear that its new possessors could survive only where there was a more or less constant supply of water.

Although Arizona and New Mexico, whose political boundaries were arbitrarily set in the nineteenth century, have much in common, they have evolved into two dissimilar cultures, the former more Anglo, the latter Hispanic. As a result, the Chicano movement has been more effective in New Mexico.

In reissuing this short yet comprehensive history, no changes were made in the text. It stands as written fifteen years ago, having been scrutinized then by those whose profession is history alone, as this writer's is not. It was written nevertheless by one with a respect for history seeking to identify the forces that have given its special character to the Grand Canyon state.

When writing in the mid-1970s, I noted the violent nature of Arizona's past, violence directed first at the original Indian tenants by the Hispanic and Anglo invaders. I observed also that this heritage is evident today in our preoccupation with Indian massacres, badmen, and shootouts in television, movies, and fiction. Our violent social behavior, today exacerbated by drug abuse, is somewhat restrained by our form of responsible self-government. Disruptive political conflicts, which threaten the social order, are moderated by our system of governance by checks and balances.

On the national scene, when presidential power became autocratic, voters restored its balancing role to the Congress. In Arizona when both legislature and governor were held by the Republican party, the voters reacted with a succession of Democratic governors from Castro, Bolin, and Babbitt to Mofford, with a Republican interlude when Mecham held power until impeached and removed from office by a coalition of both parties. Although emotions ran high, Arizona proved that it had come a long way from the days of the gunfight at the O.K. Corral.

Thus our practice of moderation restrains excessive zeal in governance. As popular a person as he was, President Reagan's appointees were sometimes forced to resign when they abused their authority. If the political aberrations of the time threw up a James Watt, whose zeal threatened to wrest our natural resources from public to private management, Arizona also sired Morris Udall, a man in the tradition of public service fathered by Hayden, Ashurst, and Goldwater.

Two more unalike politicians than Barry Goldwater and Mo Udall are hard to imagine, and yet when Arizona's welfare was threatened, they and the rest of the state's congressional delegation were quick to close ranks.

This was evident in the final drive to fund the Central Arizona Project, now nearing completion at a cost beyond that of any other federal reclamation project. Water is now being pumped and canalled from the Colorado River to the Salt River Valley to meet rural and urban needs. By 1991 it will be raised another 1,300 feet to supplement Tucson's lowering wells.

In spite of this herculean achievement, nothing has changed what was evident in 1976, that our future as a desert civilization is dangerously dependent upon a single river whose flow is subject to climatic changes. In *A River No More*, Philip Fradkin offers a sombre assessment of the Colorado's future as a life support system for Arizona and Southern California (Knopf, 1981).

What was true in 1976 is even truer in 1990. Arizona remains one of the fastest growing of the states. Because of its climate, scenery, and open space, tourism (and federal spending) are still Arizona's main sources of prosperity. In 1970 the state held 1,775,399 people. In 1980 it had grown to 2,718,215 inhabitants. The projection for 1990 of 3,600,100 indicates what might prove an unhealthy growth.

What does this mean? It means that in spite of Arizona's rank as the sixth largest state in square miles, there are too many people crowded into spaces which, because of their water supply, do not allow unlimited growth. The state's two major cities appear to be on a collision course with history. Short of desalinizing water from the nearby Gulf of California and pumping it overland, Arizona will always be an arid land, thirsting for fresh water.

Already metropolitan Phoenix and Tucson are experiencing what has degraded Los Angeles as a healthful place to live. They too will have to adopt draconian measures to reduce air and ground pollution. Back in 1900 John C. Van Dyke foresaw the threat to the desert from the newly invented automobile. Now it is the cities that are being poisoned by fumes and paralyzed by gridlock.

Arizona can still benefit from its western neighbor's lack of solutions for these ills. Needed is will and leadership. Evidences are appearing: public concern is more organized and articulate, and environmental groups multiply. Neighborhood coalitions mobilize throughout the state. All of this reflects a newly voiced national concern for a cleaner, better environment. The death of Edward Abbey in 1989 deprived the Southwest of its greatest voice of conscience. Now his books alone speak for him.

Once Arizona's leading source of revenue, together with cattle and cotton, copper has suffered from foreign competition, rising labor costs, and the mandating of stricter emission controls. Strikes, shutdowns, and smelter closings have reduced production and profits. James W. Byrkit's *Forging the Copper Collar* is an impartial history of the labor-management conflict of 1900–1921 (University of Arizona Press, 1982). Arizona suffers from being tied to the national economic health.

Tucson's hope to follow Phoenix in becoming a smokeless industrial center suffered a blow when I.B.M. came to town in 1977 and left in 1988. After the University of Arizona, the city's major employer is the Hughes Aircraft Company, whose chief output is weapons for the armed forces. Now its future is affected by the moves of the United States and the Soviet Union to reduce their armaments. Although swords can be beaten into plowshares, what useful conversion can be found for guided missiles?

The shade of Joseph Wood Krutch, one of the first to warn Arizona of unbridled growth, must be resting easier now that the Titan missile sites that ringed Tucson from 1960 were removed in 1986—all but one which earns its keep as a tourist attraction.

The arts, communications media, and higher education facilities in Tucson, Tempe, and Flagstaff have flourished, even though social services have not. Arizona remains near the bottom on lists of state spending for mental health, abused children, the homeless, and affordable public housing. The major newspapers in Phoenix and Tucson are still controlled by absentee owners. Banking is largely in California's hands. Despite my hopeful forecast that Phoenix's dynamism would produce a major novelist, even as Raymond Chandler appeared in Los Angeles, none has come. In Tucson Charles Bowden gives promise with his rapid-fire series of environmental and autobiographical books, including *Killing the Hidden Waters, Blue Desert, Mezcal,* and *Red Line.* As founding editor of *City Magazine,* Bowden cast a cold eye on the state's foibles and abuses until the magazine's funder withdrew support and the periodical expired.

The flow of books about Arizona and the Southwest shows no sign of abating. The best source of information is the monthly checklist *Books of the Southwest,* issued by the University of Arizona Library and edited by W. David Laird. Arizona and New Mexico support a wide range of book publishers and bookstores.

The two biggest cities have produced histories of importance: C. L. Sonnichisen's *Tucson* (Arizona Historical Society, 1981) and Bradford Luckingham's *Phoenix* (University of Arizona Press, 1989). Two young editors have raised their journals to a new level: Bruce Dinges's *Journal of Arizona History* and Joseph Wilder's *Journal of the Southwest* (formerly *Arizona and the West*).

Several welcome paperback reprints of reference books appeared in 1988 and 1989, including Will C. Barnes's *Arizona Place Names,* with a biographical foreword by Bernard Fontana. This is a veritable bible for travellers actual and armchair. It was followed by the *WPA 1930s Guide to Arizona* and the similar guide to New Mexico, neither as out-of-date as might be supposed. All three books were published by the University of Arizona Press, offering a printed windfall for readers.

The reference later in this volume to the unpublished manuscript by Charles W. Poston, which he addressed to the regents upon the founding of the territorial university in 1887, can now be updated. As part of the university's centennial celebration, it was edited also by Bernard Fontana, as *Lecture on Learning* and issued as a keepsake by the Friends of the University of Arizona Library. Poston's extraordinary prescience is revealed by his having urged the new school to specialize in astronomy and irrigation and to offer a special welcome to students from Mexico.

If there is a shortage of original creative art in Arizona, there is much public support of the arts on all levels. In such cultural humus, genius is fertilized. State and national support of art is a proper and healthy function of government. Painters have never been lacking in such a paintable state, although none yet rivals the chromatic genius of Maynard Dixon. Figurative sculpture has all but disappeared. A rare practitioner is John Waddell, at his studio and foundry in a remote part of the Verde Valley. His daring bronze groups grace public places from Tucson, Phoenix, and Scottsdale to Sedona and Flagstaff.

Seen more often is abstract art, which perplexes the viewer. A poem should not mean but be, said the poet Archibald MacLeish. This might be the intention of artists who fashion works without any obvious meaning. That their creations at least *are* is indisputable.

This volume closes with the epilogue "Beyond the Bicentennial," in which the writer sought to pierce the veil of the future. I refrain from ending this new preface with Beyond the Century. The weather has thickened and my turquoise ball is cloudier, prophecy in low repute, and the oracle on the far side of Baboquivari is no longer there.

And yet I will confidently predict that the 2000s will end even as the 1000s are ending, with the land of Arizona still here. What of the cities and their inhabitants? Those who can take the heat without power to temper it and with little water, will probably be here, although there is no certainty that nature will not turn on them as it has on earlier tenants. Nor should it be forgotten that their lease, like all others throughout history, is open-ended.

L. C. P.

Tucson
Bajada of the
Santa Catalinas
October 1989

Preface

HERE are many ways to write about Arizona. Mine is one that has been determined by my own predilections. I am reconciled to its not pleasing every reader, and I know that I will be criticized as much for what I've left out as for what I've put in.

Arizona is a young state in an old land. Its history goes back far beyond 1776. Peoples of several races have made its history. Some wrote it down; others had no written language. Yet all who lived here left evidences of their lives whether as hunters, planters, or builders.

We who live here now do all of these things and more. We are technologically a clever people although mostly unaware that we too hold the land in brief tenancy. In applauding our achievements as the culmination of Arizona's history, we forget that other people will come after us, and they will also be only tenants of this beautiful old land.

An Arizonan cannot live sensitively without being aware of the passage of time and peoples. The land is so permanent, the cities so ephemeral. The sky too is dominant, whether it be cloudy or blue or starry black. *Sky Determines* is the title of a New Mexico classic by Ross Calvin. It is a title also appropriate in Arizona. Here in the Southwest earth and sky tell man where he can go and what he can do.

Never a day passes that I am not aware of Arizona as a physical presence nor that I do not feel the gods around me, those gods of sky and river and earth who must be appeased if we are not to suffer their wrath. Wherever I am in the state, the Grand Canyon is also there at the back of my mind, lending perspective to my view of things. This sense of time and place and being I have sought to make implicit in the pages that follow.

A year has been spent in the research and writing of this bicentennial history which is not really a history. What is it, then? An effort by one who is a writer before he is an historian to say what Arizona was and is and may be, and also to say what seems most meaningful in our past, present, and future. No less!

Many years of Arizona experiences have preceded this one year of sustained and joyful work. My first transit of the territory came in the year of my birth, three score and ten years ago. Subsequent *entradas* and now several years of residency have brought a fond familiarity with the land and its peoples. My Arizona reading began in 1921 when a birthday present from my father was Ellsworth L. Kolb's *Through the Grand Canyon from Wyoming to Mexico*. That was my first Southwest book. It is on my desk as I write, a talisman kept near me all these years.

During the past year I have read for new information and also to test what I already knew about the state. This led to the raw and refined materials of history, to facts and folklore, and to books and archives, photographs and maps, in public libraries and private collections. Field trips have taken me around the state from Fredonia to Lochiel and from the Yuma Crossing to the Four Corners.

The round of seasons brought snow and ice, rain and flowers, dust storms and the summer monsoons. I have watched the mesquite hold back its leaves until sure that spring had come. Sweetness of *huisache*—white-thorn acacia—and the golden shower of palo verde—the Spaniards' *lluvia de oro*—have seduced me from work. Sometimes I have had to look twice to be sure the flowers of the catclaw acacia weren't yellow caterpillars. On walks at dawn and dark with our little dog Barlow, I have felt at one with all life around me.

The truth is I am a writer indoors more than out—one who has never trapped the Gila, run the Colorado, nor climbed Baboquívari. Yet those adventures *are* mine from reading James

Ohio Pattie, Major John Wesley Powell, and Justice William O. Douglas. Therein lies the magic of reading whereby every good book becomes Aladdin's lamp.

The pages that follow pass quickly over some elements of Arizona's character. I dwell little on the cultures of the Indians—Navajos, Hopis, Apaches, Pimas, Papagos, Yumas—though their reservations cover much Arizona ground. Others have described them well in such books as the ones on Indians I have recommended in the list of readings at the end. Tourists and residents alike well know that influential Indian cultures survive here, separate still from Anglo Arizona, yet inseparable from what makes the state richly distinctive.

Also familiar is much of the frontier syndrome associated with Arizona. For a long time this land was a mining frontier, a ranching frontier, and a scene of Indian troubles. Law and order came hard to the territory whose cowboy image, expressed in popular novels and films, dies hard. It is not for me to retell the stories of Geronimo, the Lost Dutchman mine, or the Arizona border rangers. Nor shall I recreate the Tonto Basin cattle-and-sheep war or the shoot-out at the O.K. Corral. I am less concerned with the violence of history than with the meaning of a violent heritage. This land was taken by force and violence, and from legends of those times came an equation of violence with manliness, and an admiration for rugged individuality, that persists in the attitudes of many Arizonans.

Has not Senator Barry Goldwater's hold on his constituents derived substantially from his association with that image? Though his forebears were men of commerce, rather than romantic frontiersmen, he is a third-generation Arizonan, a stalwart inheritor of the lands taken from the Indians by the daring and courage of the whites. And he is a spokesman for self-reliant individuality in our own time. That he may pilot a jet as often as he rides a horse only widens his appeal to the popular imagination.

Other subjects as well might have been more amply treated. But I have tried to develop in detail what I know best that best serves my purpose, trusting that such success as I may have will stimulate my readers to further venturing in the literature on our state. I hope my book will lead Arizonans down new roads to a different perspective on their history, and also persuade them to look back with pride on heroes who deserve more recognition. There are more heroes than the few I have named.

Even though the glass be dark through which we look beyond the nation's bicentennial, the mountains of Arizona are clearly there and the rivers that overflow when it rains. After our culture has gone, the desert will be there. It is heartening to know that sky and mountains, rivers and deserts, will be eternally there; and also people, one hopes, although not necessarily people of our kind, yet men and women of bone and blood and breath, even as we are.

Such is the abiding Arizona these pages seek to evoke.

Acknowledgments

When I looked at the list of those who have helped me, I saw that a sizeable appendix would be needed to thank them all. I have had courteous assistance from Arizonans throughout the state.

Initial encouragement was given by A. R. Mortensen of the National Park Service and by Patricia Paylore of the University of Arizona's Office of Arid Lands Studies. They convinced me that I was qualified to write this book.

Then it was Gerald George, the inspired editor of the Bicentennial histories, who kept me going in sickness and in health. His sustained belief and encouragement would alone have made a writer of me. The book is his as well as mine, although I alone am responsible for its shortcomings.

Colleagues at the University of Arizona who have helped me are so numerous that I can only give their names and hope to tell them personally of my gratitude for the many things they did for me. They include Phyllis Ball, James Barry, Mary Blakeley, Charles Bowden, Stanley K. Brickler, Donald C. Dickinson, Carl F. Diener, M.D., Edith H. Ferrell, Jennifer Gelder, Laurence M. Gould, Richard A. Harvill, Emil W. Haury, Jimmye S. Hillman, Harwood P. Hinton, A. Richard Kassander, Evelyn Jones Kirmse, W. David Laird, Marguerite McGillivray, Ross McLachlan, Samuel C. McMillan, Hal Marshall, Dan Matson, Angela Mendoza, Russell Munn, James E. Officer, F. Robert Paulsen, Donald M. Powell, Sol D. Resnick, Harris Richard, Mary Sarber, John P. Schaefer, Leicester H. Sherrill, Helen Sigmund, Iliana Sonntag, Alan Stein, Marshall Townsend, and Arnulfo D. Trejo.

Members of my 1975 seminar in Southwest studies aided my work in progress. Their names are Sarah Bouquet, Dana Cole, Katherine Costa, Douglas Jones, Joan Keary, Audrey Marshall, Robert Mitchell, Patrick Murphy, Rita Smith, and Donna Stephenson.

Tucsonans who aided me include David F. Brinegar, Ed Eggers, Anne-Eve Mansfield Johnson, Paul C. MeKalip, the late Dorothy Mc-

Namee, Yndia Smalley Moore, Charlotte Nusser, Don Schellie, Maria Urquides, and Leonor Mansfield Williamson.

David I. Rees of Ajo and John Charles Finzi of the Library of Congress gave me special assistance.

In the Salt River Valley help was warmly given by Carl Bimson, Marguerite Cooley, Stanley E. Hancock, R. J. Hopper, Rod J. Mc-Mullin, Edgar C. Park, John R. Schwada, Lawson V. Smith, and Joseph Stacey.

Senator Barry Goldwater's interest in my work was meaningful.

Final typing of a difficult manuscript was skillfully done by Ellen Cole and her staff.

I am grateful to Jane Whitehead for her editorial skill in preparing the manuscript for printing.

Two longtime Arizona friends were not thereby inhibited from giving my work their frank comments and editorial improvements that proved invaluable. My indebtedness transcends these words of thanks to Bernard L. Fontana, ethnologist, Arizona State Museum, Tucson, and to Bert M. Fireman, curator of the Arizona Collection, Arizona State University, and executive vice-president, Arizona Historical Foundation, Tempe.

The book's dedication symbolizes my gratefulness to my wife Fay for her proofreading, patience, and love.

L.C.P.

Arizona

1

Great Dry and
Wrinkled Land

NE has only to look down from above to see that Arizona is a deeply wrinkled old land of interminable mountains, river valleys, and desert plains. The sight of running water is rare. Dryness is obvious. Even when it rains, the thirsty earth swallows the water. The flora have learned to gulp and store, then flower and fruit and seed in the swift cycle of desert life. A man who is trying to live off Arizona's surface has to compete for his share of the liquid. Only a small fraction of the land is ever snow-covered and then for a minor part of the year. Wrinkled dryness is Arizona's dominant characteristic. Strange, intricate configurations of weathered earth form this geographically sixth largest state.

What do I mean by calling Arizona "great"? Not only for its physical dimensions, which are awesome. They range from sea level, where the mighty, long Colorado River ends in the Gulf of California, to the San Francisco Peaks, westernmost of the Navajos' Sacred Mountains, which rise to 12,300 feet above sea level, looming majestically above the ponderosa forest between Flagstaff and the Grand Canyon.

By "great" I also mean for that peerless Grand Canyon, which invites and rejects all descriptions from the grandiose to

the silly. "A good place to throw your old razor blades,"
wagged Mark Twain—or was it Will Rogers? At a jumping-off
point on the North Rim, I once saw a young couple come
laughing to the edge, look down, and fall silent. "God," the
girl finally murmured, clinging close, "is it real?" The Grand
Canyon is indeed real and great, the greatest of all water-worn
wrinkles on the face of the earth.

Yet I mean something even more. Arizona's greatness lies in
the sum total of its geography and its peoples and their efforts
from prehistoric times to come to terms with a land that makes
no concessions to human beings, caring naught that they die of
cold or heat.

By its extremes of elevation, topography, and climate, Arizona has always been hostile to man—Indian, Hispano,[1] Anglo.
Man has had to struggle to survive. Each race has fought with
the resources it had. The history of this endless struggle, not as
much to subdue as to survive, has elements of greatness com-
pounded of hardship, ingenuity, and heroism. From the simple
ditches of the Hohokam to the intricate canals of the Salt River
Project and the risen Phoenix, we perceive stages of greatness in
man's mastery of his environment.

And so across the spectrum of history are to be found different meanings in calling Arizona a great dry and wrinkled
land. I should like to accompany this book with what I have
thumbtacked on my wall. It is a three-dimensional colored map
of Arizona that shows in a glance what takes a chapter to say. It
reveals the highs and the lows, the wets and the drys—those
physical determinants of why man came to Arizona and where it
was possible for him to thrive.

Although I first learned to appreciate the role of geography in
history from a childhood love for those little blue-bound geography readers by Carpenter, it was author Bernard DeVoto who
persuaded me of the importance of air travel to the study of his-

---

1. Throughout the book I refer to Spanish-speaking Arizonans as Hispanos rather
than Mexican-Americans. Although their blood is often as much Indian as Spanish, their
language is Hispanic.

tory. If he were teaching a seminar on the West, he once declared in his column in *Harper's Magazine,* he would take his students on a flight over the great western trails—the Oregon, the Santa Fe, the Gila—so that they could see from above what can not be seen from below or gained merely from reading—could see why the westward migrations went the way they did, following the river valleys, threading the passes, and crossing the deserts to the golden land. Man walks where water flows.

During the 1940s and 1950s I often flew across the continent and came to know Arizona from the air at the same time that I came to know it on the ground and from its literature. Seen from aloft, the Mogollon Rim, a 200-mile escarpment that heralds the central valleys and lower deserts, takes on meaning not apparent from the ground. In a glance can be seen that abrupt end of the Rocky Mountain plateau.

Although my flying years are past and I go on the ground at slower speed, yet in my mind's eye I carry the relief map of the entire state, verifying it, upon homecoming, by the map on the wall.

The peaks are my beacons. Arizona lies to the southwest of the high Rockies; thus the traveler must be farther northeast to experience that transcendent sight of the great wall of mountains appearing on the horizon, heralded by their cloud cap and then by sight of their shadowy summits floating between sky and earth. It is a sight that illuminates Western literature from the explorers Lewis and Clark to Josiah Gregg, Lewis H. Garrard, Susan Magoffin, and Charles F. Lummis.

After leaving Albuquerque, the westbound traveler will at length see the first hints of the twin peaks of San Francisco, which guard Flagstaff from the north. Cloud cap signals their presence a hundred miles ahead. Then the peaks disengage from sky and earth and shimmer in the viewer's gaze. It is then that I always recall William Clark's ecstasy when he first saw the Pacific and wrote in his journal, "Ocian [*sic*] in view, O the joy!"

If it is from the west that one enters northern Arizona and climbs from the river crossing to the coolness of the Coconino

forest, there too is a welcoming mountain. It is the one called
Bill Williams that figuratively leads the traveler as it led Martha
Summerhayes a century ago when she came with her husband to
his post at Fort Whipple.

Bill Williams was named for an old mountain man who
trapped (and stole horses) on its southern slope, where the
Verde rises. Fresh from a New England upbringing and education in Germany, the young bride was indignant at the mountain's unromantic name. When she protested to her husband,
that seasoned soldier deigned to say, "I suppose he discovered
it, and I dare say he had a hard enough time before he got to
it."

During the days it took them to reach Prescott, Martha fell
under the spell of the mountain. Let her tell it:

> Our road was gradually turning southward, but for some days Bill
> Williams was the predominating feature of the landscape; turn
> whichever way we might, still this purple mountain was before us.
> It seemed to pervade the entire country, and took on such wonder-
> ful pink colors at sunset. Bill Williams held me in thrall, until the
> hills and valleys in the vicinity of Fort Whipple shut him out from
> my sight. But he seemed to have come into my life somehow, and
> in spite of his name, I loved him for the companionship he had
> given me during those long, hot, weary, and interminable days.[2]

Northernmost of Arizona's guardians is Navajo Mountain,
standing alone on the border of Utah near the confluence of the
Colorado and the San Juan. With the advent of houseboating on
Lake Powell (peace to the major's shade) this solitary peak can
now be seen from an easy chair on deck.

When I once took a long day's journey from Glen Canyon to
Kayenta, that mountain never left my sight. There it stood
through the passing hours, first in the northeast, then north, and
finally northwest, rising without foothills from the wrinkled land
to a height of 10,300 feet. Someday I'll turn off on the rough
road from Shonto and come closer to that mountain.

---

2. Martha Summerhayes, *Vanished Arizona: Recollections of the Army Life of a New
England Woman* (1908, 1911; reprint edition, with notes by Ray Brandes, Tucson:
Arizona Silhouettes, 1960), p. 48.

Far to the south of Bill Williams and the San Francisco Peaks is still another great mountain—Graham, the culminating thrust of the Pinaleños. It rises south of Safford on the Gila River, where its 10,500 feet assure visibility from a hundred miles around. This I once learned when loafing with a friend on Mt. Lemmon above Tucson. It was long ago, before the smelter at San Manuel had veiled the valley, and we could see to the east across the San Pedro to a blur of ranges, marked by one high point. "Graham," murmured my laconic companion.

Another time I rounded Mt. Graham on a long day's drive from and back to Tucson, five hundred miles in all, with that mountain as the magnetic pole. Over the San Pedro and the Gila and through Pinal Pass to Coolidge Dam and Lake San Carlos I traveled, then on up the Gila, with that mountain looming closer.

At Safford came the turn to the south. Above me rose the bulk of Graham, wearing its cap of cloud, as if truly a blue-shouldered abode of the gods. As I joined the El Paso road, the mountain stood in the north, as it did most of the way back to Tucson—the Old Pueblo. Then far to the southwest appeared the last of my mountain lodestones—helmeted Baboquívari, sacred peak of the Papagos, which dominates the borderland with Mexico.

None of these Arizona mountains are rock climbers' mountains to rival the Rockies or the Sierra Nevada. The first recorded climber of Baboquívari was Robert H. Forbes, early university professor, chemist, agriculturist, hydrographer, and state legislator, who died in 1963 at the age of 101. His first ascent was in 1899. He enjoyed it so much that he made it an annual event on his birthday. When his legs finally gave out, the old man asked to be flown to the summit by helicopter.

Justice William O. Douglas was Baboquívari's most famous climber. His beautiful account of the ascent appeared in *Arizona Highways*.[3] Edward Abbey has also written of the view from the summit. "When I was there," he wrote in *Cactus Country*,

3. *Arizona Highways* 27:16–25 (April 1951).

"I could see about half of southern Arizona and quite a parcel of Mexican Sonora and a lot of mountains: the Santa Catalinas, the Ajos, the Huachucas, the Agua Dulces and the Pinacates and others down in Mexico. When the air is clear, I've been told, you can see the waters of the Gulf of California, some one hundred and fifty miles away by line of sight." [4]

Why do I dwell on these high points of Arizona? Not as much for their recreational, economic, and ecological importance, which is indeed great, as for their ability to excite the imagination as symbols of the power and the glory of this land.

It is not enough that they be sacred only to the Indians. If we are to be more than material possessors of the land (albeit transients), if as a people we are ever to rival the greatness of our land, we must recognize that there is a power that cannot be measured by our instruments. Martha Summerhayes sensed it in her awe of Bill Williams Mountain. There is eternal meaning in the Psalmist's words "I will lift up mine eyes unto the hills from whence cometh my help."

On the façade of a capital building in one of our neighboring states are carved the words "Give me men to match my mountains." That is indeed a lofty demand in a state which includes the peaks of Shasta, Lassen, and Whitney. Here in Arizona may our mountains also serve to measure our leaders.

The rivers that flow from Arizona's mountains are the lifeblood of this arid land. Their water is also our help. Greatest of all, not only of Arizona but of all the west, is the Río Colorado. This red giant gathers its power in a succession of tributaries, among them the Gunnison and the Green, the San Juan, the Little Colorado and the Virgin, the Bill Williams and the Gila. The water they drain from the western slope of the Rockies flows through canyons, turbines, and desilting basins to the Gulf of California—at least what is left after vegetation and people have taken all they require to live.

4. Edward Abbey, *Cactus Country* (New York: Time-Life Books, 1973), pp. 104–105.

This old chasm-carver also carries "bad water" between Arizona and California. Although our neighbor contributes nothing to it, yet the Golden State is the Colorado's chief beneficiary. Through aqueduct and power line the river has nourished Southern California to giant size. While the people in both states increase, the river's water does not. Conflict is inevitable.

Arizona's greatest benefits have come from a stream other than the Colorado, a tributary once removed of the big red river. Phoenix in the desert owes its life to this smaller river the Spaniards called El Río Salado—the Salt. Since the construction in 1911 of Theodore Roosevelt Dam, first of the Bureau of Reclamation's major flood and irrigation projects, the Salt River Valley has grown into perhaps the greatest urban district between Chicago and Los Angeles. This miracle was wrought by water that belongs to Arizona alone.

The water unused by Phoenix and the valley reaches the Colorado via the Gila, into which the Salt empties. Although it rises in southwestern New Mexico on the western slope of the Continental Divide, the Gila's great length lies in Arizona. It flows across the state, gathering the waters of the San Francisco, San Carlos and San Pedro, the Salt, the Verde and the Hassayampa, to join the Colorado above Yuma. Precious little water is left beyond Painted Rock Dam. Along its sandy length the river wears a green belt of cotton, alfalfa and grain, vegetables, melons and citrus.

Among these rivers of Arizona there is none to impress an Easterner used to the perennial flow of the Hudson, Connecticut, Susquehanna or Delaware. And a Midwesterner from the banks of the big three—Ohio, Mississippi, and Missouri—would laugh if told by a Tucsonan that his city lies on the shores of the Río Santa Cruz.

Southernmost of the Gila's tributaries, the Santa Cruz and the San Pedro flow north from the higher borderlands of Mexico. Their water is seen only when they are flooded in the rainy seasons of winter and summer. Then they are not to be crossed.

Because so much of its water is used for irrigation, the Santa Cruz rarely reaches the Gila today. That poor stream sinks out of sight and is seen no more. The Santa Cruz is an odd river. Although it rises in the grassland southeast of Tucson and flows first into Mexico, it soon changes course and fishhooks around to disappear in the desert beyond Casa Grande.

The San Pedro shows more certainty. Rising in Mexico near the border below Bisbee, it flows north to reach the Gila near Winkelman. Both the San Pedro and the Santa Cruz were once perennial rivers, heavily wooded and lushly grassed. Overgrazing and erosion and the demands of agriculture have changed their nature and habits.

One other river flows north northwest. The Little Colorado rises in the central mountains and brings life to Springerville, St. Johns, Holbrook, and Winslow; then it crosses the Painted Desert to reach the big river near the head of the Grand Canyon. The early Mormons settled along its course.

Arizona's rivers were once untamed. In flood they ran wild, in drought they all but disappeared. Only the mighty Colorado kept on flowing in all seasons. Until dams checked their rampages and stored their waters against drought, the rivers of Arizona were their own masters.

Thus we see that Arizona's river system is an odd one. The stream with the most water is the least usable for Arizona's needs. Most of the Colorado's course in the state is through inaccessible, barren land. Even when it comes to form the border with California, it does the least good to Arizona because the lower elevation of the western side means that the coastal state benefits from gravity flow, whereas the water for Arizona must be pumped to the higher elevations. Hence the controversial Central Arizona Project to pump water up to the lands around Phoenix and Tucson, which, by the time its diversion facilities are fully funded and constructed, may find the river bled dry by users in the Upper Basin.

I have referred to Ross Calvin's book about New Mexico called *Sky Determines*. Its thesis is that the state's cultures come from its heavenly climate. This is also true of Arizona. Water falls from the heavens in the form of rain and snow. Mountains capture this moisture, store and then yield it in springs and streams. One has only to go to a mountain headwater to see it happening. There melt, seep, and drip coalesce into rivulet, brook, and stream, all mingling in the roundup of the waters—*El Rodeo de las Aguas.* Rivers are formed, which flow toward their lowest level. All the waters of Arizona flow toward the Gulf of California.

Whence comes Arizona's sky water? In winter it arrives in storms from the Pacific, in great weather fronts spinning down counterclockwise from the mother of storms, the Gulf of Alaska, to saturate the Pacific Northwest and northern California, then dwindling as they move southeast, occasionally drenching semiarid Southern California, finally to be milked dry by the mountains of north and central Arizona, which return the moisture to earth in snowmelt and runoff.

This is an immemorial cycle known to Arizonans time out of mind. In Frances Densmore's *Papago Music,* we find her translation of a song sung by the Papagos when they set out on their annual salt-gathering expedition to the coast. When questioned, the informants told her that in their opinion the sea holds everything—the clouds and the wind. The storms come from the sea and spread over the world, and the clouds follow after, so they think there is some connection between the sea and the rain. Here is her translation of this old Papago weather song:

> By the sandy water I breathe in the odor of the sea,
> From there the wind comes and blows over the world.
> By the sandy water I breathe in the odor of the sea,
> From there the clouds come and rain falls over the world.[5]

Tucson is on the fringe of these storms, receiving only enough rainfall to tide the arboreal desert over until the summer rains begin—those monsoons of moist tropical air, which blow in from the gulfs of Mexico and California with high drama of

---

5. Frances Densmore, *Papago Music* Smithsonian Institution, Bureau of American Ethnology. Bulletin no. 90 (Washington: Government Printing Office, 1929), p. 173.

lightning and thunder and turbulent air. Phoenix receives even fringier benefits. The poor-weather relative is the desert from Gila Bend to Yuma. There neither winter nor summer brings any relief to the parched earth.

Thus if Arizona has one master word of description it is *dry*. This great state is, first and last, an arid, semiarid land, which no amount of flowing prose can make into a permanent paradise. Lawns and links are artificial here, conventional flower gardens a waste of water. The farsighted Arizonan adapts to his environment and seeks not to adapt it to his own pleasure.

Although their engineering skill is incomparable, the Anglos have much to learn from the Indians of the sacredness of water. "What they [the Indians] worship most is water," observed an unknown chronicler with Coronado in 1540, "to which they offer painted sticks, plumes and powders made of yellow flowers, this usually at springs. Sometimes they offer such turquoises as they have." Coronado himself reported to the viceroy, "The water is what these Indians worship, because they say it is what makes the corn grow and sustains their life." [6]

Four centuries have passed, and still the Indians of Arizona acknowledge the divinity of water. Up north the Hopis employ serpentine rituals to bring down rain. Down south the Papagos sing for power over the precious element.

What do Anglos do? We dam rivers, build canals and aqueducts, tap underground sources; we even seed the clouds fruitlessly. Our engineers and atmospheric physicists seek to work these wonders. In their unthinking acceptance of their liquid bounty, our people merely turn faucets and let water run and waste. If we acknowledge the sacred peaks as symbols of help and sources of power, how, then, should we deify water? My answer is that we should render homage to water with fountains, with symbolic constructions of stone and metal. The good medi-

---

6. Herbert E. Bolton, *Coronado on the Turquoise Trail; Knight of Pueblos and Plains* (Albuquerque: University of New Mexico Press, 1949), p. 131; *"Relación del Suceso"* in George P. Hammond and Agapito Rey, *Narratives of the Coronado Expedition* (Albuquerque: University of New Mexico Press, 1940), p. 286.

cine thus made would offset the loss of water from evaporation. Let every city, town, and village in this dry and dusty land dedicate a fountain to the source of life. Let the children be taught from the cradle that water comes from beyond the faucet, comes from the sky gods, however defined. We might then return to a lost state of grace.

Such, then, is our great dry and wrinkled land of Arizona, a land of mountains, rivers, and deserts, made by wind and water into strange and beautiful configurations from Grand Canyon, Painted Desert, conifered mountains, and junipered mesas to irrigated valleys and waterless wastes. This weathered chunk of earth has now been peopled and made productive. To what end? And for how long?

People have lived in Arizona through many millennia and may still be living here when the Ice Age returns and calls time. Is Phoenix the last of the miracles to be wrought in this old land?

2

The Procession of
Her Possessors

ALTHOUGH Arizona has been long possessed by man,
no race has held it for very long. Writing of another western
land that has also known a succession of occupants, the poet
Robinson Jeffers declared of the Carmel coast of California,

> The soil that I dig up here to plant trees or lay foundation stones
> is full of Indian leavings, seashells and flint scrapers; and the
> crack-voiced church bells that we hear in the evening were hung in
> their tower when this was Spanish country. Where not only genera-
> tions but races, too, drizzle away so fast, one wonders the more
> urgently what it is for, and whether this beautiful earth is amused
> or sorry at the procession of her possessors.[1]

No one knows how long man has lived in Arizona. Twelve to
fifteen thousand years is a low estimate. Prehistoric man left
few records other than the bones of the large animals he hunted
and the killing weapons and butchering tools that he used. Such
evidences were unearthed by Emil Haury in Ventana Cave on
the Papago Reservation, a hundred miles west of Tucson, and
along the San Pedro southeast of the city. They may be seen

---

1. S. S. Alberts, *Bibliography of the Works of Robinson Jeffers* (New York: Random
House, 1933), pp. 50–51.

today in the Arizona State Museum on the campus of the University of Arizona, reminders of man's earliest possession of the land.

With the retreat of the Ice Age, the big animals disappeared. In order to survive, their hunters had to adapt to plant foods. They became gatherers. They had always gathered; now it became more essential and in time was supplemented by planting. Around 2000 B.C., the archaeologists believe, cereal grains, squash, and beans were brought into Arizona by peoples from Mexico. The Arizonans gradually became sedentary agriculturists—when there was enough water. Their problem is ours, four millennia later, of how to live on a land with a meager and irregular water supply.

These early Arizonans can be differentiated by the major environmental zones—desert, mountain, plateau—into the three cultural groups by which we identify and classify them: Hohokam, Mogollon, and Anasazi. All have left their history in the form of archaeological records.

On the northern plateau dwelled the cliff people of Keet Seel, Betatakin, Canyon de Chelly, Chaco and Frijoles canyons, and the Coloradan Mesa Verde, and later the lonely Hopis on their three barren mesas. More haunting than the museum evidences of the earlier flesh eaters are the abandoned cliff dwellings of these Anasazi (a Navajo word meaning "The Ancient Ones"). They were intended for defense against enemies.

Spruce Tree House on the Mesa Verde, White House in Canyon de Chelly, and remote Betatakin and Keet Seel (which play a role in the early Arizona-Utah novels of Zane Grey)—the mere sight of these erstwhile dwellings transfixes the gaze of the traveler and mesmerizes his imagination until he becomes convinced, as I once was, that the dwellers are still there and may be seen on the ladders and in the rooms, grinding, potting, and making nets to catch small game.

In her *Land of Journeys' Ending* Southwestern author Mary Austin wrote of this "residue of personality left in all places once inhabited by man," and of her reaction to "some trace that human sense responds to, never so sensitively as where it has long lain mellowing through a thousand years of sun and silence.'' [2]

Such evocations may be found throughout Arizona. In the Verde Valley and in the forested mountains of the upper Gila are other defensive cliff dwellings. By A.D. 1400 marked changes occurred that ended the Anasazi culture. The causes are obscure. Some believe that inroads of raiding Comanches, Navajos, and Apaches were responsible. Another likely cause was a drought of thirty years when scant snow or rain fell and the streams ran dry. Tree-ring dating shows that there was such a drought between 1270 and 1300, although it may not have occurred with the same intensity throughout the whole region.

Along the Salt and the Gila the canals of the desert dwellers we call the Hohokam were gradually filled with sand, and their culture came to an end. *Hohokam* is a Papago word meaning ''all used up'' or ''people who have gone.'' Their lands were probably exhausted by an overuse of water rather than by drought, by the rising to the surface of alkali from their practice of saturation irrigation, and so they kept drifting downriver to more fertile soil. What finally became of them? No one knows for sure. Some believe that there is a connection between them and today's Pimas or Yumas.

A single ruined building is virtually all that remains of the subsequent Salado culture—the Casa Grande, a strange four-story rammed-adobe structure built about the time of the long drought and then abandoned. Was it a temple? A granary? An observatory? Those river people first came into Arizona from the south, bringing perhaps some vestiges of the Mayan religion. The Casa Grande is now a national monument, protected from the elements by a steel canopy. It is as eloquent a testimonial to man's transiency as the Egyptian Sphinx, and recalls those lines of Shelley:

2. Mary Austin, *Land of Journeys' Ending* (New York: Century Co., 1924), pp. 385, 65–66.

My name is Ozymandias, King of Kings.
Look on my works, ye Mighty, and despair.

Along the Colorado River no enduring Indian culture was ever established although river people are still there. There were various reasons. The tribes from Yuma to the Grand Canyon were constantly at war with each other. The Colorado was wilder than the Gila, either too deeply engorged or, in its lower reaches, too overwhelming in spring flood to allow social stability along its banks.

In one way or another it was water that made the early possessors of Arizona only temporary lords of the arid lands. Their medicine failed. They lacked the techniques to utilize the Colorado, whose endless flow came from snowy, saturated watersheds far distant.

All the while the northern Navajos and Apaches were penetrating into Arizona, thrusting even deeper into Mexico for slaves, and gradually becoming the rulers of all but the driest southwest corner. This they were generally content to leave to the bean-eating Papagos and the squash-and-melon-fed Yumas and Mojaves.

Then came still another wave of possessors. The Spaniards arrived toward the middle of the 1500s, their lust for gold and slaves whetted by the fall of Mexico to Cortez. Back to Spain their galleys wallowed, riding low in the water from the weight of golden plunder. In 1536 Cabeza de Vaca, with Estevan the Black Moor and a few other survivors of a shipwrecked crew of 400, wandered into the Mexican village of Culiacan after an eight-year odyssey from the beaches of Florida.

Did these men cross a corner of Arizona, thus gaining place in history as the first white men to enter our land? No one knows, but at least they came close. There were no boundaries then. Their tales of golden cities to the north set the Spaniards off on a search for this fresh source of riches.

They were led by Don Francisco Vasquez de Coronado along an equivocal route that probably followed the San Pedro into

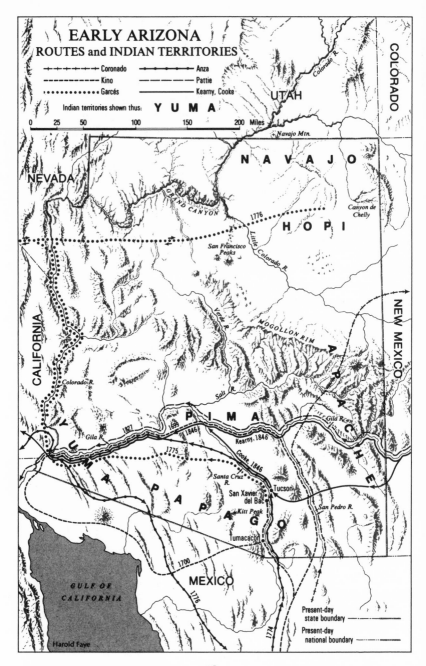

EARLY ARIZONA
ROUTES and INDIAN TERRITORIES

+++++++ Coronado   •—•—•—• Anza
- - - - - - Kino   - - - - Pattie
•••••••••• Garcés   ———— Kearny, Cooke

Indian territories shown thus: **Y U M A**

0   25   50   100   150   200 Miles

COLORADO

UTAH

NEVADA

N A V A J O

Navajo Mtn.

Colorado R.

GRAND CANYON

1776

Canyon de
Chelly

H O P I

San Francisco
Peaks

Little Colorado R.

Verde R.

NEW MEXICO

MOGOLLON RIM

CALIFORNIA

Colorado R.

Salt R.

A P A C H E

Gila R.

1827

P I M A

1699

Gila R.

Kearny, 1846

Y U M A

Gila R.

1846

1775

Cooke 1846

P A P

Santa Cruz
R.

San Xavier
del Bac

A   G O

Kitt Peak

Tucson

San Pedro R.

Tumacacori

1700

GULF OF
CALIFORNIA

1776

MEXICO

1774

Present-day
state boundary ————

Present-day
national boundary - - - -

Harold Faye

18

Arizona to a point near today's Benson. There they would have crossed over the Galiuros into Aravaipa Valley and northward through Eagle Pass in the Pinaleños below Mt. Graham. They might have crossed the Gila at Bylas and gone on into the mountains to the land of the Zuñis and beyond as far as what is now Nebraska. Growing up in the western part of that state, Willa Cather heard tales of those first Spaniards of long ago and from them made the story she called "The Enchanted Bluff."

Coronado's quest was in vain. For all their lust the Spaniards found the fabled golden cities to be only pueblos made of mud. And so Arizona was written off. New Mexico was a more likely province for colonization and Christianization, if not for gold. This was because of its geography, which differs so radically from that of Arizona. Instead of barrier ranges angling across the land and rivers either inaccessible or subject to extremes of dryness and flooding, New Mexico is favored with one great central valley, an unimpeded north-south corridor running the length of the land and watered by a mostly accessible perennial river whose source lies in the eternal snow of the Colorado Rockies. It was an easy roadway north toward the persistent dream of riches despite Coronado's failure. Men of God led the second *entrada* north to a golden harvest of heathen converts.

The Río Grande flows with a gentle gradient, affording a secure livelihood to the pueblos along its shores. Their inhabitants proved more likely converts than any to be found in Arizona. The Spaniards were first welcomed by the Indians along the Río Grande as allies in the defense against the raiding Comanches and Navajos. Although there was no gold, there was green life along the river. And so the Spaniards stayed and intermarried with the Indians. This admixture gave New Mexico its character, which endures to this day, an Hispano-Catholic-Indian culture not established in the adjoining land of Arizona except among Pimas and Papagos. The basic reason was the lay of the New Mexican land and its great river-roadway of life.

Although Arizona was a part of Spain and then of Mexico until the United States possessed most of it in 1848, it never became truly Hispanic. Its very name is Indian, not Spanish, that of a Papago place, Arizonac, meaning "Little Spring." Its greatest Spanish missionary was not Spanish at all, but an Italian named Eusebio Chini who had received a Jesuit education in Austria. The only thing Spanish about him was the Hispanization of his name to Kino. He never wanted to be assigned to missionary work in Mexico. The Orient was his goal. There in the 17th century the Jesuits had made a deep impact on science and learning. When he drew lots with a fellow priest to see where they would go, Kino lost. Thus he came to glory in Sonora in northern Mexico.

As Father Kino he is known to this day, the greatest Arizonan of early time in the magnitude of his achievements as explorer, cartographer, astronomer, developer of agriculture and animal husbandry, and founder of Christian missions among the Indians. Kino came to the Pimería Alta (northern Sonora and southern Arizona) in 1687. There he labored until his death at Magdalena in Mexico in 1711.

A fellow padre described Kino in these words: "He prayed much, and was considered without vice. He neither smoked nor took snuff, nor slept in a bed. He was so austere that he never took wine except to celebrate mass, nor had any other bed than the sweat blankets of his horse for a mattress and two Indian blankets. He never had more than two coarse shirts, because he gave everything as alms to the Indians." [3]

Unlike Coronado and his cohorts who came for gold, Kino came for God. His missions sought self-sufficiency by his introduction of grains and livestock. He was a peacemaker, not a warrior. A prodigious man on horseback, his *entradas* throughout the quarter century of his mission ranged to the utter limits of the Pimería Alta, from the San Pedro to the Colorado and from the Concepción to the Gila. His feats of endurance have never been equaled. It was he who explored and mapped the

3. Juan Mateo Manje, *Unknown Arizona and Sonora*, translated by H. J. Karns (Tucson: Arizona Silhouettes, 1954), p. 263.

Mar de las Californias, or Sea of Cortez, and who first showed that Baja was a peninsula and not the island delineated on earlier maps. *"California no es isla"* were his words.[4] No other man in the history of the Spanish Southwest approaches Kino in humility and strength.

Yet the quest for gold impresses men more than the search for God. Thus in *Arizona Place Names* Coronado receives eight entries to one for Kino. Now in our time, thanks to the research and writings of Herbert E. Bolton, Frank C. Lockwood, and the Jesuit historians, Kino is newly honored in Arizona and Sonora with schools, hospitals, and even land developments bearing his name. In 1974 the presidents of Mexico and the United States met in Magdalena de Kino, Mexico, to pay homage to him whose bones are buried there.

In Washington's Statuary Hall Kino stands as one of two Arizonans, although it and other statues of him in Phoenix, Tucson, Nogales, and Hermosillo are idealized likenesses. He was too busy, too humble a man to sit for his portrait. Both of these qualities, if not the correct raiment or spelling, are best seen in the monument by Ralph Hume which stands in a park on the northern approach to Nogales.

Our early history is essentially the biographies of such heroes as Kino. To this day in Arizona, when we are more than ever needful of heroic public figures, Kino is a lasting prototype, a man of devotion, intelligence, and compassion, who stands on our threshold as an inspirer.

The temporal work of Kino and his fellow Jesuits was tragically undone in 1767 when, for political reasons, the Spanish Crown expelled the order from all lands under Spain's dominion. Kino's missions soon fell into ruin. They extended into Arizona along the Santa Cruz; Guevavi, Tumacácori, Bac, all were abandoned to the ravaging Apaches.

The Franciscans then came into the Pimería Alta, and there

---

4. Herbert E. Bolton, editor, *Historical Memoir of Pimería Alta*, 5 vols. (Berkeley: University of California Press, 1919) 1:342–348.

was a slow rebirth of missionary zeal. The mission San Xavier del Bac, called the White Dove of the Desert, was rebuilt in the form we know today. Its pastor during the reconstruction was a true Spaniard named Francisco Garcés, a native of Aragon, Spain's northernmost province. He took up his mission at the Papago village of Bac in 1768 when he was thirty years old. Like his Jesuit predecessor he was an explorer, equally hardy, heroic, and compassionate, and determined to bring the grace of God to the heathen.

Unlike Kino, Garcés was not an organizer, a rancher, an administrator, or a scientist. He was a devout "loner," compulsively on the move, down the Santa Cruz and the Gila, up the Colorado, traveling with mule and sometimes a Pima guide and interpreter. More often he went alone, content to squat on his heels and share the Indians' greasy fare around a campfire. His spartan zeal carried him down the Havasupai trail to the bottom of the Grand Canyon over a route he found as perilous as the pass of Canfranc in the Pyrenees above his natal province.

On the day when our independence from England was officially declared at Philadelphia—on the Fourth of July in 1776—this lone Franciscan was far west at the pueblo of Oraibi, come there on muleback to convert the Hopis to Christianity. They turned him away. In that day's entry in his diary we read what happened:

July 4. As soon as day broke, I heard singing and dancing in the streets; the route passed by where I was, and then only did I see that some of the Indians were painted red, with feathers and other decorations on the head, beating the sound of the dance on a kind of drum with two small sticks, to which the flutes played an accompaniment; and many persons kept time to the music as well through the streets as on the housetops. The sun having now risen, I saw coming nigh unto me a great multitude of people which caused me some fear of losing my life. There came forward four Indians who appeared to be principals, of whom the tallest one asked me with a grimace, "For what hast thou come here? Get thee gone without delay—back to thy land!" I made them a sign to be seated, but they would not. I arose with the Santo Cristo in my hand, and partly in Huma, partly in Yabipai, and partly in Castillian, with the aid of signs, which are the best language to use with Indians, I explained to them my route, naming the nations whom I had seen, those who had kissed el Cristo; I told them that all these had been good to me, that I also loved the Moquis, and for that reason I came to say to them that God is in the sky, and that this señor whom they saw on the cross was the image of God, who is good. To this responded an old man in Castillian language and making a wry face, "No! No!" Then I said, "Fetch my mule!" After a little, the Yabipai youth appeared with her, and, having arranged my things, I mounted on her back, showing by my smiling face how highly I appreciated their pueblo and their fashions.[5]

On an earlier journey to the Colorado at Yuma, Garcés concluded that Alta California, colonized by the Franciscans in 1769, could be reached overland from Pimería Alta instead of by the rough sea passage from Mazatlán. Back at Tubac on the Santa Cruz he reported his belief to another Spaniard who ranks among the heroes of Arizona. He was the captain of the presidio, Juan Bautista de Anza, a native of Sonora as his father was before him, a soldier-administrator possessed also of the compassion often lacking in professional warriors.

Persuaded by Father Garcés's report, Anza sought the ear of Viceroy Bucareli in Mexico City and persuaded him that an overland exploration was in order. Accordingly in January 1773 Anza, Garcés, and thirty-four soldiers marched to the Colorado-Gila confluence and there, by a show of target shooting and prayers, induced the hostile Yumas to pledge fealty to crown and cross. And of more immediate importance, to ferry them across the river.

The Yuma chief was christened Captain Salvador Palma. Least known and appreciated of the Indians of the Southwest, this Yuma leader made possible the bridgehead and gateway to California; and although his abused people were to rise a decade later and massacre the rapacious colonists at Yuma, it was

---

5. Francisco Garcés, *On the Trail of a Spanish Pioneer,* 2 vols. edited by Elliott Coues (New York: Harper, 1900), 2:388–390.

Palma who sought in vain to spare the life of his friend Garcés who had founded the mission there.

Now in 1773 the small band of Spaniards pressed on over the honey-colored dunes, desert, and mountains to Mission San Gabriél in Southern California, thus establishing the first overland route from Sonora.

Anza's report to Bucareli resulted in the approval of a major emigration of colonists from Sonora and Sinaloa. After marshaling at Tubac, the great company set out for Alta California in September 1775. Included were 240 men, women, and children; 695 horses and mules; and 355 cattle; supported by a great variety of equipment and supplies.

So masterfully had Anza organized the expedition and so firm was his leadership that all arrived safely in California save for one woman who died in childbirth soon after leaving Tubac. With Anza himself as midwife, two more babies were born en route, and all three infants survived the trek.

Again the river crossing was made possible by Captain Palma's goodwill. It was celebrated by a feast of watermelons to the number of two thousand, dug from sandy storage where the Yumas were wont to keep them. In the diary of Garcés's fellow priest, Pedro Font, we find an amusing account of his failure to persuade Palma's nubile daughters (both nimble swimmers) to wash the red paint from their naked bodies. " 'You wash us!' they demanded and, lo, he did!'' [6]

After settling the colonists at Monterey, Anza pressed on with a few soldiers to found what became the presidio of San Francisco.

Not only did Anza report his success to Bucareli, he also took Palma with him to Mexico City, wearing the colorful costume sent him by the viceroy. Anza's reward was the governorship of New Mexico, where in a decade of arduous service he succeeded in repulsing the Comanche threat to the colonists and puebloans of the Río Grande. New Mexico's gain was Ari-

6. Herbert E. Bolton, editor, *Anza's California Expeditions,* 5 vols. (Berkeley: University of California Press, 1930), 4:496.

zona's loss. The tragic events at Yuma would never have occurred if Anza had remained in Arizona and the viceroy's promises of gifts been honored. Thenceforth Palma fades from history.

Nor was there peace along the Santa Cruz. The Spaniards had settled athwart the old Apache raiding trail into Sonora. There was plenty of water then. The river followed a green course down the valley to the Gila. The deeper Papaguería would have been safer terrain for settlement, but there was not enough water there. The Spaniards called it *El Camino del Diablo*—The Devil's Road. Kino had passed that way.

After his decade of Indian fighting in New Mexico, Anza returned to command the presidio at Tucson founded in 1775. His days were numbered. He died at the age of 53. Nowhere does his name appear on the map of Arizona, nor that of Garcés in any significant instance. We should reorder our hero priorities and enlarge our hall of fame.

Mexico won independence from Spain in 1821, and the door was thereby opened through which the United States would eventually force its way to the Pacific. Manifest Destiny, it was called. The initial trade with Mexico, celebrated in Josiah Gregg's *Commerce of the Prairies,* led from the Missouri-Kansas frontier to Santa Fe and thence south to Chihuahua. The American and European demand for beaver pelts for men's hats sent the mountain men trapping the rivers of the Rockies and beyond. The Gila and all its tributaries to the least creek were worked, and then the trappers pressed on to the Colorado and its feeders, and upriver from the Gila confluence until blocked by the Grand Canyon.

All the streams of the Southwest were then wooded and willowed and banked with grasses. It was a rich land, Indian land, teeming with grizzly bears. In a single day Trapper James Ohio Pattie sighted 250 of them. (He was given to exaggeration; it might have been only 25.) When the Indians attacked the intruders for their goods, coffee, flour, and whiskey, the trappers fought back, wanting only to escape with their own hair and their packs of beaver pelts. The land itself they did not want. When the Mexicans, who were being harassed by the Apaches, placed a bounty on Indian scalps, some unscrupulous mountain men found quicker returns for hair than for fur, caring naught whether they scalped the Mexicans themselves. Any scalp, dried until unrecognizable, brought the promised bounty.

It was a time of treachery, violence, and bloodshed. There were massacres by Anglos, one of which, said to have been witnessed by Mangas Coloradas (Red Sleeves), the Mimbreño Apache chief, led him to a vow of vengeance. In such incidents lay the origins of the long war to subdue the Apaches. The 1820s and 1830s were decades of cruel conflict throughout the Southwest, only rarely lightened by any incidents of pathos and compassion.

Pattie tells of one incident in which an Indian camp was decimated save for an old man who went on eating his bowl of mush. He proved to be blind and deaf. Another time the trappers found a hastily abandoned camp whose only occupant was a crawling, squawling baby. They secured it by a rawhide string. It was later retrieved by its parents, who left a deerskin as a thankful token. Whereupon the trappers left them a red handkerchief.[7]

Only a conventional war with killing done by rules could curb the outbreaks of individual savagery. Such was the war of 1846 between the United States and Mexico whereby with the subsequent Gadsden Purchase the entire Southwest, except for Sonora and Baja, was swept into the Union as either state or territory.

Indian, Spanish, Mexican—such was the procession of Arizona's possessors. And then a little more than a century and a quarter ago, the United States seized the land. Now to see what we have done with it and what it has done to us, and what our possession of it has meant for the Union.

7. James Ohio Pattie, *Personal Narrative*, edited by M. M. Quaife (1831; Chicago: Lakeside Press, 1930), p. 223.

3

Confrontation and Conflict

NOT long after the United States had won its independence from England, the westward movement began to gather force. Jefferson perceived its inevitability, and by the Louisiana Purchase he removed the French obstacle. He also sent Lewis and Clark on their way to the Northwest, leading to the eventual elimination of the British and Russians from that rainy coast.

The second greatest territorial expansionist was President James K. Polk, whose term of office was from 1845 to 1849. Like Jefferson he personified the doctrine of Manifest Destiny— to possess the continent "from sea to shining sea."

Polk's hope was to acquire the Southwest from Texas to California by diplomatic negotiation with Mexico. This was not to be. Mexico's victory over Spain had inflated her national ego, and she regarded herself as invincible. On paper her army was superior to ours in numbers, training, and equipment. France was thought (wrongly, it proved) to be a ready ally.

The war with Mexico came in May 1846, precipitated by our annexation of the Republic of Texas and a subsequent Mexican attack across the Río Grande. By August it was all over. Civil strife throughout Mexico prevented any concerted war effort. Yet ours was not a bloodless victory. Several savage battles were fought deep in Mexican territory. Many young lives, Mexican and American, were lost.

Although the settlement two years later by the Treaty of Guadalupe Hidalgo included Arizona north of the Gila as part of the ceded territory, the war itself had no effect in Arizona. What was there to be affected in that raw land? Aside from the Indians, the population numbered a mere 600, mostly Mexicans. Tucson was a miserable presidio, garrisoned by a few ragged troops who lived in fear of the Apaches, the real rulers of the land. Once the beaver were trapped out, the Americans had no desire for Arizona above or below the Gila. Mining, livestock, lumbering, agriculture, were yet unknown. Kino's missions along the Santa Cruz and down into Sonora were long since secularized and fallen into ruin. San Xavier del Bac was used as a cattle barn and granary. The Franciscans had gone. The land was either too hot and dry or too snowy and cold. There were no roads to link it with the United States other than the Gila Trail, made known by Pattie's sensational narrative. Neither country was concerned either to invade or defend Arizona. It lay beyond the pale, untouched and unconcerned by the war, its future veiled. California was the prize, and New Mexico lay on the way to the coast. It already numbered 30,000 inhabitants dominantly Hispano-Indian as against Arizona's few non-Indian settlers.

And yet the future of Arizona was determined by the war even before it ended in the victorious annexation. It began with President Polk's dispatch of Colonel Stephen W. Kearny and his Army of the West to hasten overland and seize both New Mexico and California. The British and the Russians were believed hovering off the coast, ready to land and claim.

New Mexico fell without a shot being fired when Governor Armijo decided the better part of valor was to yield to Kearny. The American leader then split the Army of the West into four parts. One remained at Santa Fe to consolidate its hold on the country. Another proceeded to Mexico to join up with General Zachary Taylor's forces. A third was led by Kearny posthaste to California. The fourth, a battalion of Mormon volunteers recruited for President Polk by Brigham Young in exchange for their pay going into the meager church coffers, was placed under Kearny's ablest officer, Lieutenant-Colonel Philip St. George Cooke, and ordered to establish a southern wagon road to California.

This route was the Gila Trail. Arizona's destiny emerged from its blazing. The discovery of gold in California two years later led to the greatest overland rush of all time as thousands of argonauts stampeded over this and the northern trails to the diggings. A more southerly route was followed by Cooke in order to avoid the rocky canyon of the upper Gila, down which the first trappers had come.

The crossing by Cooke and his motley Mormons with wagons and animals was an heroic achievement. Kearny's was also a great feat although on a lesser scale, as he was persuaded by Kit Carson to leave his wagons behind. With a strike force stripped to a hundred picked dragoons and mule-drawn cannon, Kearny made it down the upper Gila over a route unsuited to even the four-wheel-drive vehicles of today. He was accompanied by Lieutenant William H. Emory of the army's Topographical Engineers Corps, whose subsequent report is a remarkable document.

Cooke's scouts, including Pauline Weaver and Baptiste Charbonneau, were mountain men who had been over the route only on horseback, and only one of whom, Antoine Leroux, remained sober. Their problem was the ancient one of the Southwest: water. The four hundred men and their mules, and the cattle and sheep that were driven along for food, required a large daily ration of water. Where was it to be found? No one knew for sure. There were no accurate maps. They had to scout ahead and aside and even to dig for it.

And there was no road, no road at all over which the men and wagons could travel with any uniform speed. We have only to look at the land today as the highway carries us smoothly over it. Hills have been blasted through, arroyos filled, and all made easy. Even the Romans, greatest of road builders until the Age of the Bulldozer, never equaled our transcontinentals.

With pick and shovel, ropes, muscle and sweat, the Cooke caravan dug and tugged and cursed its way west. Its achievement resembled Anza's, three-quarters of a century earlier. Yet Cooke did not exert the discipline that made Anza such a strong leader. His Mormon volunteers were reluctant soldiers, several times on the verge of mutiny and prone to break their vow of abstinence from alcohol. At one point Cooke was forced to order them to unload their muskets.

As a professional soldier he managed to rule the rough band and hold them on course. Coming down the Río Grande when he realized that they were heading into Chihuahua, he rose in the saddle and called a halt. "This is not my course," he roared. "I was ordered to California," and with a mighty oath, "I will go there or die in the attempt." Turning to the bugler he ordered him to blow the right. Whereupon the battalion wheeled west "through a wilderness where nothing but savages and wild beasts are found," Cooke reported, "or deserts where, for want of water, there is no living creature." [1]

After crossing Coronado's trail of three centuries earlier along the San Pedro, Cooke learned that the Mexicans still occupied the presidio of Tucson, as they were to do for another ten years. After a token show of resistance, they did as Armijo had done at Santa Fe and let the Americans take possession. The few civilians shared their flour and meal, fruit and tobacco. Tucson reminded Cooke of Santa Fe. The ruinous Mission San Xavier del Bac could be seen across the plain, even though it was not until our time that its walls and towers were given their dazzling whitewash.

After a brief rest Cooke rallied his command and down the Santa Cruz they went, men, mules, wagons, and livestock, bound anew for Californy. Upon reaching the Gila they found

---

1. Ralph P. Bieber, editor, *Exploring Southwest Trails* (Glendale, Cal.: A. H. Clark, 1938), p. 108.

the Pima villages friendly. "I rode up to a group of girls," Cooke wrote in his journal, "naked above the hips. It was a gladdening sight. One little girl excited much interest with me. She was so joyous that she seemed very innocent and pretty. I could not resist tying a red silk handkerchief on her head for a turban." [2]

The gold seekers who came in the wake of Kearny and Cooke also found these Pima villagers ready to trade foodstuffs for implements. They were given to stealing, however, with especial fondness for unguarded mules.

Down the Gila the battalion marched to the Colorado, and here, in addition to an eye for nubility, Cooke showed a sense of humor. In the dead of winter the mile-wide river was fringed with thin ice. When one boatload of the Mormons was having trouble poling its way across and began to drift downstream, Cooke, who was on the west bank, mounted his horse, waved his hat in farewell, and shouted, "Goodbye, gentlemen, when you get to the Gulf of California, give my respects to the folks." [3]

Then came the dunes, the desert, and the mountains where one narrow, rocky pass proved so impervious to pick, shovel, and axe that the wagons had to be taken apart and carried through in pieces.

Cooke reached San Diego on January 29, 1847, after four months en route. California was already in American hands, although it had cost Kearny eighteen of his dragoons, lanced to death by the Mexican Californios at San Pasqual.

Cooke was unimpressed by the country through which his men and wagons had passed. The roadway that his orders commanded him to build was what mattered. He had extended the Santa Fe Trail by more than a thousand miles. Although first called Cooke's Wagon Road, the route came to be known as the Gila Trail. "Marching half naked and half fed, and living upon

2. Bieber, *Exploring Southwest Trails*, p. 170.

3. Odie B. Faulk, *Destiny Road* (New York: Oxford University Press, 1973), p. 26.

wild animals," Cooke concluded his report to Kearny, "we have discovered and made a road of great value to our country." [4] He was right. To this day it remains one of the main routes to California.

Although a native Virginian, Cooke remained loyal to the Union and served out a long, honorable career in the army, dying in 1895 at the age of 85. Today in Salt Lake City one of the few Gentiles to be honored by a statue is Philip St. George Cooke, leader of the Mormon Battalion.

Because the Treaty of Guadalupe Hidalgo used a faulty map to establish the boundary between the United States and Mexico, a strategic strip, including that stretch of Cooke's Wagon Road between Mesilla and Tucson, was disputed by the United States and Mexico. The planners of the railroad west saw it as vital for their route.

When the Gadsden settlement proposed that the line be moved south to where it would have been if the Disturnell map had been accurate, loud was the outcry in Congress against paying Mexico $15,000,000 for a worthless piece of scrubby desert. One senator even said that if he were acting as a private citizen he was confident that Mexico would sell him the strip for $6,000. Compromise was reached on a price of $10,000,000, and in 1854 the boundary was redrawn as it is today except for adjustments made by the shifting beds of the Río Grande and the Colorado.

Again because of its remoteness and general undesirability Arizona was untouched by the Civil War. Although it was first seized by the Confederates, and its scant population centered in Tucson was predominantly "Secesh," Arizona soon fell to the Union forces from New Mexico and California. A few skirmishes were all that it took. Since 1850 Arizona had been a part of the Territory of New Mexico. In 1863 President Lincoln

4. Odie B. Faulk, *Arizona, A Short History* (Norman: University of Oklahoma Press, 1970), p. 64.

signed a Congressional act establishing a separate territory, which it remained until 1912 when it became the forty-eighth state.

The rising tide of Manifest Destiny, set in motion by the Confederates, who saw Arizona as the road to a Pacific port for what they anticipated would be a permanent and coexistent Confederate States of America, flowed on through in the debacle of Confederate hopes.

Only the Indians remained antagonistic. They fought long and hard to hold their land and feed their gnawing bellies. If it had not been for the Gold Rush and the subsequent opening of southern Arizona by traffic over the Gila Trail, the Apaches would have kept their hunting grounds and raiding routes for a longer time. Mining, cattle raising, ranching, and trading saw the land grow ever more populous and yield richer booty to their raiding. The Apaches found that it took less time and effort to loot the nearby Gringos than the more distant Mexicanos. Inevitably the United States Army was called upon to protect the American settlers. It took the army longer than a generation to subdue the Apaches.

There were few heroes on either side. Today the Apache chieftains are enshrined in the pantheon of folklore more by fiction, movies, and TV than by history. They include Mangas Coloradas, the Mimbreño Apache whose lands lay in New Mexico up near the headwaters of the Gila. There the copper deposits at Santa Rita del Cobre bred conflict between his people and the miners. Mangas's years on the warpath began when he was flogged by the miners at Piños Altos, although this is disputed by some historians. His death was the result of treachery.

Mangas's peer was Cochise, the Arizona Chiricahua Apache whose desert land lay athwart the Gila Trail. Another act of treachery triggered Cochise on the warpath, although raiding was the traditional Apache way. They were not farmers, gatherers, or hunters of the meager game. The Apaches were professional, incomparable raiders.

And so blood flowed for several decades. As Apache hopes

waned, the lesser chieftains Victorio and Geronimo grew more desperate, cruel, and wily, fighting and running to the end, which came in the 1880s when the last of the Apache warriors were shipped to Alabama and Florida.

Best known of the army leaders was General George Crook, who respected his foe and fought him with honor. No spit-and-polish brass hat, Crook wore a duster over his uniform and rode hell-for-leather. In *Vanished Arizona* we glimpse him in these words of Martha Summerhayes: "One day a party of horsemen tore past us at a gallop. Some of them raised their hats to us as they rushed past, and our officers recognized General Crook, but we could not, in the cloud of dust, distinguish officers from scouts. All wore the flannel shirt, handkerchief tied about the neck, and broad campaign hat." [5]

Those Apaches who left the warpath rather than die were settled on the reservations of San Carlos, along the middle Gila where Coronado had crossed, and of Fort Apache, higher in the White Mountains above the Mogollon Rim.

Apache Agent John P. Clum is another of the few Americans of the period who rank with General Crook as effective in dealing with the Apaches. Although his charges had given up the fight, it took little to break them out again on the warpath. Clum has also entered history as the founding editor of the *Tombstone Epitaph* and by his provocative journalism became the impresario of the gunsmoke and bloodshed of Tombstone.

Today the San Carlos Apaches are not a happy lot. The tribe is split into factions fighting over money. Alcohol is their poison. Wickiups bearing TV antennae are a common sight, as well as women in brilliant garments bending over washing machines. University researchers have encouraged the Apaches to harvest the wild jojoba bushes for their oil-rich seeds. The Whiteriver Apaches are better off with resources of tall timber and tourist concessions for hunting, fishing, and camping. Fort Apache itself, now an Indian school, remains much as it was

5. Summerhayes, *Vanished Arizona*, p. 54.

when the Summerhayeses were posted there and Martha bore her first child under primitive conditions.

Confrontation and conflict were also the lot of Arizona's largest tribe, the Navajo, whose lands spread over the northern plateau. Before the Spaniards introduced livestock, the Navajos were gatherers and raiders. With the coming of the Americans under Kearny, the long-suffering *pueblenos* of the Río Grande were promised protection from their predatory neighbors. There were punitive expeditions into Navajoland.

When the Civil War distracted the army, the Navajos increased their raids. As a result Colonel Christopher Carson, better known as Kit, was ordered in 1863 to subdue them by destroying their crops and livestock. Thus in March of 1864 began the Long Walk of their deportation. Destination was Fort Sumner southeast of Santa Fe where a band of Mescalero Apaches was restrained. Only children and cripples were allowed to ride in the wagons. All the rest, eventually eight thousand of them, trudged the three hundred weary miles, accompanied by their sheep and goats and horses. There are few more despairing chapters in our history. Only the most defiant and hardy succeeded in hiding out, holed up like foxes in the depths of the Grand Canyon and the San Juan and on the Black Mesa and Navajo Mountain.

Their exile endured for four years while these proud Navajos, who called themselves *Diné,* "The People," languished in captivity, penned on a barren military post in that monotonous part of New Mexico. There they were ravaged by smallpox in an epidemic that killed more than two thousand. They stubbornly refused to build dwellings other than their traditional hogans.

When strong protests finally availed in Washington and the Navajos were allowed to return to their homeland, their societal equilibrium had been destroyed. With token help from the government in the form of livestock and seed, they began to rebuild their way of life, concentrating on a pastoral existence, since the U.S. Army's strength precluded their former raids into the valley of the Río Grande.

Then in the 1880s the railroad proved another kind of intrusion, followed in our time by the automobile. These forms of transportation brought the Americans with new diseases, raw whiskey, and some unscrupulous traders. An exception was Don Lorenzo Hubbell, whose trading post at Ganado became a symbol of success. It is now a national historic monument, its records preserved in the university library at Tucson.

The zeal of some Christian missionaries was matched by their insensitivity to the Navajos' religion. The Franciscan father Bérard Haile was a noble exception. Out of this dark night of misguided well-meaning came such impassioned books as Oliver La Farge's *Laughing Boy*. In this romantic love story of a young Navajo couple, Laughing Boy and Slim Girl, the author portrays the destruction of the ceremonial Indian ways by the encroaching Anglos.

High on their rocky mesas, enclaved within Navajoland, the Hopis suffered mostly from Navajo encroachment and thievery. The Americans sought persistently to change their immemorial religion even as Father Garcés tried but failed to do centuries before.

There is a large literature about the Indians of Arizona, a small literature by them. Because they left no written records, we cannot know the details of their lives during the centuries when they possessed the land. Their surviving artifacts, arts, and ceremonials reveal their essential nature. They lived closer to the earth and more in harmony with the elements than we do. In their adaptation to this land of sun and sky and water they dwelled in a state of grace. Yet they were not free from violence. Nature was hostile in flood and drought. We romanticize their existence as idyllic. It was not. There were many hazards. Food had to be hunted or cultivated, and it was never in certain supply.

Arizona's Indians were not mere savages. They evolved their own magic and religion, practiced artful crafts, and created poetry. They made good medicine by ceremonials that persist to this day, although the ceremonials have been adulterated by Hispanos and Anglos with their alien religions.

The Apaches were raiders. They were also artists with a sense of design and decoration that wedded form and function. Their basketry illustrates this. In the museum of the Amerind Foundation in the Dragoon Mountains a hundred miles east of Tucson is a display of Apache basketry that heightens our admiration of this creative people.

An inspired work of fiction gives more insight into life than a pedestrian work of fact. The novel *Apache* by Will Levington Comfort, which I shall discuss at length in a later chapter, is a necessary corrective to the lurid literature about these Indians. Better than any work known to me, *Apache* conveys a sense of what it was like to be displaced by a more ruthless and efficient race.

Now in the bicentennial year of 1976 we seem to be at a watershed time, with history beginning to flow the Indians' way. A new sense of social justice—of righting old wrongs—that quickened in the administration of Franklin D. Roosevelt and was personified by Indian Commissioner John Collier, has intensified until we see a movement among the Navajos for autonomy as a nation within the nation.

Is it possible? What are the implications for the other tribes? Can thus be righted the wrongs done the Seminole, the Sioux, and the Cherokee? The Navajos now have strong medicine in royalties from oil, gas, and coal. Yet where do riches alone lead a people? Where have they led us? Are we Anglos any happier now than the Navajos were before we destroyed their ceremonial ways? Can the Indians' present culture, blended of theirs and ours, ever be other than bastard? The modern Navajo outdoes the Anglo in his passion for air-cooled pickup trucks, Tony Lama boots, booze, and bureaucracy.

If this greatest Indian state were to have strong and inspired leadership, there might come from it a prototype for social living whereby other minorities could thrive. Yet along the railroad in Navajoland, along the Gila and the Colorado and deep in the Papaguería, amenities alone have not brought happiness to the Indians any more than they have to the Anglos. Alcohol, homicide, and suicide are often the concomitants of progress. Wherever whites and Indians have mingled as they have along the rivers, railroads, and highways of Arizona, the Indians are the ones who have suffered most from disease and decadence. *Laughing Boy* is more than a novel. It is a lament for beauty lost.

Ethnologist Bernard L. Fontana is a friend of the Papagos, long resident with his wife and children on land adjoining the San Xavier Reservation. We should ponder his words:

> Perhaps we need other measures of progress than those which can be defined in terms of money and the things money can buy. An expensive new home is simply an indifferent artifact. If its residents have lost dignity and hope and have become forlorn, the home is meaningless as a symbol of success. No less so for us than for Indian people.
>
> This is not to say that material wealth bodes evil or disaster. It is how we control and who is controlling the production, distribution, and consumption of that wealth that are important. Unless we can define "progress" in our own terms and can make decisions in our own behalf based on our own priorities of needs as well as on an understanding of the possible ranges of alternatives, it is difficult to see how there can be human progress in anyone's terms. We have laid our notions of progress on Indians, and we, rather than they, control the means. The Indian reaction is an understandable one. And it is proof again that the power to define is the ultimate power.[6]

Conflict can result in destruction alone, or it can strengthen men to new creative effort. The Americans possessed Arizona by conflict and destruction. They vanquished its previous owners, Mexican and Indian. Today they dominate the land. Yet through the century and more that it has been an American possession, Arizona has come to be known as the Copper State and the Grand Canyon State. Thus its popular image is of the land itself rather than of its people.

6. Bernard L. Fontana, "Progress on an Indian Reservation," *Progress and History in Arizona,* edited by W. R. Noyes (Tucson: University of Arizona, 1973), unpaged.

4

Long Night of the Territory

WITH the increasing number of Americans who came after the land was theirs, Arizona entered into its long territorial night. It was a kind of political limbo in which the president of the United States appointed the governor and other high officials and in which its one delegate to Congress was voteless. For the first thirteen years Arizona was a part of New Mexico, then in 1863 it became a territory of its own.

More is needed to make a land truly a people's land than a stroke of pen, even though that stroke were made by President Abraham Lincoln. Arizona was the Indians' land for countless millennia regardless of the lack of any written laws of ownership. It was their land because they lived on it in harmony with its nature, their lives determined by its configurations, seasons, and weathers. On the high plateau, in the forested mountains, and on the seedy deserts they lived by planting and gathering or by hunting and raiding—by ways of life mostly foreign to those who displaced them. Although poor in goods, austere in habits, predatory and often cruel, the Indians were nevertheless compatible with their domain.

Then suddenly it was no longer theirs. Their land was ours. Who were we? What did we want of the land? Today we mine and ranch and farm it, we make and buy and sell things to each other. Thousands have come to Arizona to enjoy a life of leisure. How did it all come about? What led to our complex state of work and play as the present owners of Arizona?

The Spaniards came for glory, God, and gold, and were disappointed in their desires. The trappers skinned out the beaver and left. The argonauts rushed through on their way to the gold fields. The Gila Trail was no more attractive to them than it was to Philip St. George Cooke. It was a road on which Arizona was only a way point, mostly dry and barren and, at places such as Tucson, merely squalid. California was the goal of thousands in a hurry who saw nothing in Arizona to stay for. Their desire was fixed on the farthest west where they had heard that gold lay in lumps for the gathering.

Not everyone suffered from this lust that swept around the world. A few emigrants perceived that Arizona, though it had some gold, held other riches—silver and copper. When some failed to strike it rich in California, they returned to Arizona and dug in there. Those who hungered for land saw wealth along the grassy rivers and in the tall timber of the middle highlands. Others prospered as sutlers, providing food and liquor, clothing and supplies to the soldiers who were fighting the Indians.

Once the land had status and protection as part of the United States, its development began. The territorial Arizonans did not come for political liberty or religious freedom. Those had been won in 1776 and earlier. Arizonans then and now are Arizonans mainly for materialistic reasons, to make a living or to enjoy a living made elsewhere. Like the rest of the western lands, Arizona was "up for grabs."

"It is not surprising," said Howard Lamar, best of the territory's historians, "that Arizona's few pioneers were topographical engineers, army officers, mining and railroad promoters, filibusters, merchants, and sectional politicians." He explained further:

> Except for the Mexicans already there, the bona fide settler was conspicuously absent. Yet while it was a frontier artificially

created by public policy and sectional interest, the Arizona story cannot be understood without also remembering that the Americans were so overwhelmed by the California Gold Rush experience that they constantly dreamed of repeating that saga in other mineral-rich areas. The devotees of Manifest Destiny firmly believed that this investment of the public treasure would be repaid tenfold. From 1848 to 1860, then, Arizona was a no-man's-land, into which the golden hopes, the expansionist dreams, and the sectional fears of the United States were projected with extraordinary vigor.[1]

During this long territorial night there were few whose desire was for anything other than self-service and gain. Most of the early profits from mining went elsewhere. Except for the missionaries and such selfless military men as Anza and Cooke, early Arizonans were a grabby lot. There was no one among them to match Brigham Young, who led his people into the wilderness to establish a religious center.

When we search the recent past for heroes to people Arizona's hall of fame, there are few to choose from. First is the man who called himself the Father of Arizona—Charles Debrille Poston. If he was a hero, as I perceive him, he was not a conventional one. He was an aggressive, imaginative, someways idealistic adventurer given to conviviality, hyperbole, and much bad luck. A Kentuckian with a glib tongue and a sure sense of his own destiny.

Though rebuffed at the polls and denied political preferment, though reviled by secessionists as a Union man in spite of his Southern origin, Poston remained an inalienable Arizonan. Complex in character, mixed in motives, with puckish humor and exuberant imagination, "Colonel" Poston is a shining figure in those dark years of mostly self-serving men. "A very agreeable and cultivated gentleman," Martha Summerhayes found him.[2]

He was a young law clerk who came to California in the Gold

1. Howard R. Lamar, *The Far West, a Territorial History* (1966; New York: W. W. Norton, 1970), pp. 430–431.

2. Summerhayes, *Vanished Arizona*, p. 168.

Rush as a federal job holder, determined to live by his wits rather than by pick and shovel. From 1851 to 1853 he was the chief clerk in the San Francisco Customs House.

News of the Gadsden Purchase launched Poston on an argosy of intrigue and adventure involving Mexican land grants, railroad routes from the Mississippi to the Pacific, and lost silver mines. He was gregarious, persuasive, and daring. A combination of those qualities brought him finally to Tubac, where in the abandoned Mexican presidio he established himself as the alcalde of a silver-mining company, empowered by the territorial government of New Mexico "to celebrate the rites of matrimony, baptize children, grant divorces, execute criminals, and declare war."

There Poston ruled as a patriarch unchallenged until Archbishop Lamy sent his vicar from Santa Fe to investigate these unorthodox goings-on. It cost him $700, Poston romanticized, to adjust the matrimonial situation whereby Father Macheboeuf sanctified the unions blithely celebrated by Poston.

This was surely the strangest community in Arizona's history. The territory was in deepest limbo. The Mexicans had left, and the New Mexican government was far away in Santa Fe. "We had no law but love," Poston's fantasy recalled, "and no occupation but labor. No government, no taxes, no public debts, no politics. It was a community in a perfect state of nature." In this frontier utopia, while silver was being mined in the nearby Santa Ritas, Poston proceeded to print his own Tubac currency on the same handpress from which issued Arizona's first newspaper, the *Weekly Arizonian*. In a report of 1856 to the eastern stockholders of the Sonora Exploring and Mining Co., Poston expressed grand hopes, which he lived long enough to see realized although his personal fortunes went into a long decline. He wrote loftily of the Tubac venture:

> It is an enterprise which has for its object the noblest aims and involves not merely the acquisition of wealth for its projects but the reclamation and employment for the purpose of civilization, of the richest and the wealthiest of our territory—a territory which

shall add to our national greatness and make our country more emphatically what we now fondly boast it to be: the greatest, wealthiest, and freest of the globe.[3]

Alas for him, the Civil War brought an end to Poston's dream world. When the protective troops were withdrawn, the Apaches moved in for the kill, and Tubac was reduced to rubble.

Poston was in Washington when the time came to make Arizona a separate territory. By so doing, New Mexico saw a way to rid itself of the Apache menace that was rendering its western reaches untenable. President Lincoln was favorable. He recognized that even as California's gold was aiding the Union, so might Arizona's silver also help defeat the South.

Poston's nimble tongue led to his being chosen, so he said, to lobby Arizona's cause before the president and the Congress. Lincoln sent him to the key legislators. "O yes," said Senator Wade of Ohio, "I have heard of that country—it is just like hell. All it lacks is water and good society." [4]

There was opposition in Congress. One member declared that the territory in question was already hopelessly overrun by red savages and Confederate sympathizers. Fortunately the majority saw with Lincoln an opportunity of gaining mineral wealth for the Union, and so the bill passed the Senate by 25 to 12, was signed by Lincoln, and became law on February 24, 1863. The proposed name of Gadsonia was discarded in favor of Arizona, which had been in use for several years.

At his own expense of $1500, Poston commissioned Tiffany's to make a sculpturesque inkstand of Santa Rita silver, bearing his name and Lincoln's, which he presented to the president upon the signing of the bill. He claimed later to have organized an oyster supper to celebrate the victory. When he learned that Lincoln had appointed a group of lame-duck con-

---

3. Charles D. Poston, "Building a State in Apache Land," *Overland Monthly* (1894), 24:207. Reprinted Tempe, Arizona: Aztec Press, 1963.
   4. Poston, "Building a State" p. 403.

gressmen as the officers of the new territory and that it was they who flocked to eat his oysters and drink his champagne, Poston was chagrined. "As I was apparently to get nothing but the shells," he recalled, "I fortified myself with a drink and exclaimed, 'Well, gentlemen, what is to become of me?' " [5]

Whereupon they made him superintendent of Indian Affairs. His appointment, dated March 12, 1863, was signed by Lincoln.

Writing thirty years later in the *Overland Monthly* and signing himself as president of the Arizona Historical Society, Poston recalled homely memories of the martyred leader:

> President Lincoln was always accessible amid his heavy cares. As my family lived in the neighborhood [Hardin County, Kentucky] where the president had been reared, my little girl made him a satchel of corn shucks from the field where he had hoed corn barefooted in the briars, thinking he might appreciate a souvenir from his old home. One afternoon I escorted my daughter to the Executive Mansion to deliver the present. The president received it graciously, and made enquiries about the old neighbors.[6]

Not too unhappy, Poston set out for Arizona, traveling by overland stage to Sacramento, then by riverboat to San Francisco. There he met an old friend, J. Ross Browne, also an intellectual adventurer, who had served in various government offices in California. Poston talked Browne into joining him in another mining venture in Arizona, not only for Browne's knowledge of Indians but also because he was an artist and had newspaper connections. Poston saw in him a press agent as well as an illustrator of mining sites for a promotional prospectus.

This encounter resulted in one of the best of the early travel books about Arizona—Browne's *Adventures in the Apache Country*. With illustrations from the author's own sketches, it was serialized in *Harper's Monthly Magazine* before appearing as a book in 1868.

Their travels took them back over the Gila Trail to Yuma and

5. Poston, "Building a State" p. 404.
6. Poston, "Building a State" p. 408.

Tucson and past ruinous Tubac to Sonora and the Papaguería. Poston's official position afforded them a small military escort against the Apaches. Along the way Browne made bold and beautiful drawings—an Apache crucified by the Pimas, Piman basketry, the Painted Rocks on the Gila (now a state historic site), the peak of Baboquívari, and the silvery Santa Ritas. A self-portrait of him drawing with a rifle across his knee was wryly captioned "The Fine Arts in Arizona." His account of their travels was lively and satirical, humorous and serious, a civilized, if biased, account of a barbaric country.

Tucson drew Browne's scorn as "a city of mud boxes, dingy and dilapidated, cracked and baked into a composite of dust and filth; littered about with broken corrals, sheds, bake-ovens, carcasses of dead animals and broken pottery; barren of verdure, parched, naked, and grimly desolate in the glare of a southern sun." [7]

Its inhabitants fared no better. "If the world were searched over," he wrote, "I suppose there could not be found so degraded a set of villains as then formed the principal society of Tucson." He was able to report, however, that the Union forces from California had somewhat ameliorated the pueblo's abject condition. [8]

Browne saw that until the Apaches were contained there could be no successful development of the territory. While the Pimas and Papagos were praised for their friendliness, Browne believed that the Apaches must be exterminated. In spite of this one extreme judgment, Browne was otherwise no subscriber to the belief that "the only good Indian is a dead Indian." He had moments of compassion as in this passage written while he was encamped along the Santa Cruz at the time of the Civil War:

When we turned in upon our soft, grassy beds, and looked up at the clear star-spangled sky above us, there were some among us, I

7. J. Ross Browne, *Adventures in the Apache Country,* edited by D. M. Powell (Tucson: University of Arizona Press, 1974), p. 131.

8. Browne, *Apache Country,* p. 134.

have no doubt, who thought that a home in such a charming wilderness would not be unpleasant, if one could be assured of such peace among men as reigned over the quiet earth. But peace like that is not for the races that inhabit this world. I lay for hours thinking over the unhappy condition of our country, and a profound sadness oppressed me as vision after vision of bloodshed and suffering and death passed like some funeral cortege through the silent watches of the night. Far away, friends were falling in sanguinary strife; everywhere God's beautiful earth was desecrated by the wickedness of man; even here, in this remote wilderness, we were not exempt from the atrocities of a savage foe.[9]

Browne returned to California on receiving word of family illness, and continued his search for government preferment.

What became of Poston? He zealously served the territory as its first delegate to Congress from his firsthand knowledge of its nature and needs. In a memorial to Congress he urged the creation of a Colorado River Indian reservation, with provision for river navigation and irrigation of the bordering lands. The army's efforts prevented its adoption. The army's prime objective was to contain the Apaches.

Poston's star fell with Lincoln. He was defeated in 1865 for re-election, because of his failure to return home and campaign. It was the same fate that befell Arizona's Senator Henry Fountain Ashurst in the next century. Then, after J. Ross Browne became minister to China, he remembered his old friend, and Poston was sent on a quasi-official mission to study agriculture in the Orient. This led him to India, Egypt, and Persia, where he became enthralled with the sun-worshiping sect of Parsees. He then lingered in London in search of backing for another mining project.

It was ten years before he returned to Arizona, this time as Register of Titles in the U.S. Land Office at the new settlement of Florence, population 500, on the middle Gila. "It was a severe contrast with London, New York, and Washington," Poston remarked in his diary.

9. Browne, *Apache Country*, p. 263.

His office was a cube of adobes measuring fifteen feet by fifteen feet. There, with time on his hands, Poston turned poet. In wretched doggerel he wrote an allegorical epic called *Apache-Land,* and in 1878 had it published in San Francisco at his own expense. Poston was blunt about his poem. "It was written in a mud hut," he declared, "on a dirt floor; without the advantage of a single book of reference, with no more knowledge of metrical composition than a donkey has of a yard stick; and it goes into the world a simple child of the desert like the author." [10] The frontispiece was his own portrait.

The collector-historian, H. H. Bancroft, said of *Apache-Land,* "This is a poem not without merit, though some of the rhymes and measures would make an Apache's hair stand on end." [11]

Poston's poem is an odd work, a mishmash of history, Indianology, archaeology, and sardonic comment on the author's contemporaries, leavened by sly humor. Here is a sample of this curiosity of Arizona literature:

> Fair Florence, wreathed in Gila's green,
> A city yet to be, I ween.
> Green cottonwoods adorn the banks,
> And no where 'neath Italia's sun
> Can climate equal such a one.
> The Gila's silvery waters flow
> Through the town, as classic old Arno
> Flows through fair Italia's Firenze,
> Enough to give a poet frenzy.
> The Pinal range ten leagues to north
> Is where the silver ores come forth,
> For pious, good, God-fearing men—
> Who drink a little now and then. [12]

While stationed at Florence, Poston sequestered a butte on the edge of town and renamed it Primrose Hill after London's high-

10. Charles D. Poston, *Apache-Land* (San Francisco: A. L. Bancroft, 1878), p. 3.

11. H. H. Bancroft, *History of Arizona and New Mexico* (1889; facsimile edition, Albuquerque: Horn and Wallace, 1962), p. 517.

12. Poston, *Apache-Land,* pp. 138–139.

est elevation. He employed Indians and Mexicans to build a wagon road to the top, and there they blasted deep foundations for a sun temple to serve as his own tomb. Poston's Folly, it was called.

The rest of his life was a series of disappointments. His frequent petitions to the president to be named governor were ignored. A few sops were thrown him. "In 1890," he wrote in a manuscript found after his death, "I returned to Arizona as agent of the Department of Agriculture and have been in Phoenix ever since—sometimes with a Christmas dinner, sometimes without. It does not matter much whether you get a dinner or not in Arizona. The eternal sunshine warms the body and the soul—for those who have a soul. It is my country's and God's. I came here in youthful days for causes which are nobody's business; and here I shall die and be buried." and he continued:

> In the course of my peregrinations, I have attended all kinds of religious worship practiced by mankind and have drunk all kinds of liquors which have been distilled or fermented for his solace or restoration; and taken in moderation, they are all good, some better, some worse. It does not matter what kind of liquor you drink so it is for the benefit of your health; and it does not matter what kind of religion you practice so it is for the benefit of your soul.[13]

As consular agent in Nogales, military agent in El Paso, reporter on artesian wells for the Agriculture Department, and superintendent of the university's Agricultural Experiment Station, Poston eked out a meager living. Along the way he founded historical societies in Arizona, the first in Tucson and, when he fell out with it, another in Phoenix. It was Poston who first urged the preservation of the Casa Grande. Before ostrich plumes came into fashion, he suggested establishing an ostrich farm at the base of his butte. His proposals for irrigation projects on the Gila and the Colorado came eventually to pass.

Back for a time in Washington, he spent his days in the Read-

13. A. W. Gressinger, *Charles E. Poston, Sunland Seer* (Globe, Arizona: D. S. King, 1971), p. 183.

ing Room of theY.M.C.A., and there he composed a series of lectures on Learning and Religion and dedicated them (together with the copyright) to the regents of the newly founded University of Arizona. They were never published. The manuscript reposes today in the university's library.

In 1899 the territorial legislature granted Poston a pension of $35 a month. He had become a tatterdemalion, cadging drinks and telling tales of bygone days when he was the alcalde of Tubac. His meager table was shared with a pack of stray dogs.

Poston died in squalor at Phoenix in 1902 at the age of 77. Twenty-three years passed before the state's conscience was moved by State Historian J. H. McClintock to dig up his supposed remains and rebury them, with official ceremony, under his pyramidal monument on Piimrose Hill. A copper plaque, since vandalized, courtesy of the New Cornelia Copper Co., Gen. John C. Greenway, General Manager, identified Poston as "The Father of Arizona." The monument is now guarded by the sheriff of Pinal County—at least by his short-wave radio facility—at the end of a road inaccessible to ordinary vehicles.

During World War II the name of Poston was given to a camp on the Colorado River where 20,000 Japanese-Americans were concentrated. Today Poston, Arizona, consists of one building, used by Indians as a crafts center.

Why have I given so much attention to this Arizonan Quixote? Because he personifies the mixture of motives—materialistic and idealistic—that attended our beginnings. His dreams ended in dust. He failed to leave any more than his name as an example of high-minded failure. Yet there are lessons to learn from his life. A young generation is rising in Arizona with its own definition of success, a definition blended, as Poston sought to blend his career, of materialism and idealism. I commend him to that generation.

The capital of Arizona Territory was established north of the Gila near Fort Whipple at a new townsite named Prescott after the historian. In this single act was fixed the enduring Anglo character of Arizona, so radically different from the mother territory of Hispanic New Mexico. Wooden buildings painted white rather than earth-colored adobes gave Prescott the look of Ohio rather than of Sonora. Here Arizona was proclaimed American, not Mexican, Unionist, not Confederate. Although the capital was moved later to Tucson, then back to Prescott, and finally to Phoenix in 1889, where it remained, the power of Arizona was lastingly vested north of the Gila, safe from possible corruption by Sonorans or unreconciled Confederates.

There followed a procession of territorial governors none of whom qualifies for my pantheon. Of them Richard P. McCormick (also known as Slippery Dick) was the most literate and capable. He founded the first newspaper in Prescott and then in Tucson, where the *Daily Citizen* is today Arizona's oldest continuously published journal. It was he who named Prescott. Arizona's destiny would probably have been realized earlier if McCormick had remained in the territory.

Ablest of the governors was Anson P. K. Safford, McCormick's chosen successor, who established the public school system. When John C. Frémont was given the governorship as a political reward, he established only token residence in Tucson. These and other governors moved on to greener pastures. They resembled the carpetbaggers who invaded the South after the Civil War. As historian Lamar makes clear, like the other western territories Arizona was governed by a frontier oligarchy, a federal ring, wherein the public officials were also the private entrepreneurs. Law and order and a measure of social stability were established. Thus public good and private gain were achieved in a generally profitable working arrangement.

For a century copper has been Arizona's dominant (and some say domineering) metal. Although silver and gold are still mined, copper is king. More than half the nation's supply comes from Arizona. Until recently copper was the state's major single source of income and taxes. Now it has been overtaken by the manufacturing industries that flourish in Greater

Phoenix. Although there are huge unmined copper reserves in the state and methods of mining are being improved, the sources of energy upon which mining depends are diminishing. So there is uncertainty in the future.

Copper is not for lone prospectors. The mining, extracting, and smelting of copper ore is profitable only after an investment of millions of dollars. Thus after a beginning by a few intrepid entrepreneurs, Arizona copper became the province of corporate business. Economic power is political power. Corporate control of government by the mines and the railroads characterized Arizona's early development and was the basis for law and order. The Wild West of Tombstone, Tucson, and Nogales was the lawless result of an unstructured, amorphous society so bitingly reported by J. Ross Browne and others. Where copper ruled, there was a more tranquil society.

Empires of corporate power and control usually begin with powerful individuals. When we look back at the beginnings of Arizona copper and the rise of the great metal companies symbolized by Phelps Dodge Corporation (or simply P.D.), we discern two legendary figures, one a hero, the other a villain.

The hero is a man who had to live for half a century before he achieved success. Dr. James Douglas came to personify Arizona copper by routes that led from his birth in Quebec as the son of a famous Canadian doctor and historian, to theology and medicine and finally to metallurgy. The latter field was arrived at by chance. After his father had lost money in a Canadian copper venture, young Dr. Douglas was led by a flair for chemistry to investigate the process of ore extraction.

Then in middle age his winning number turned up. In collaboration with another scientist he discovered a new method of extraction, which led to his association with a Pennsylvania copper venture. A New York company of metal dealers by the name of Phelps Dodge sent him to the wilds of Arizona to report on a copper claim at Bisbee.

Thus came Douglas to Arizona. It was the glory road that led to the greatest name in Arizona's mining history—the Copper

Queen mine—and to the growth of Phelps Dodge into the monarch of Arizona copper companies. Dr. Douglas's genius flowered in all aspects of the operation—mining, smelting, industrial organization, and humanitarian concerns. He achieved the highest professional honors in American mining and metallurgy. A spare-framed, gentle, tenacious Scotch-Canadian who never relinquished his allegiance to the British Crown, his fate was to be overshadowed by the company whose triumph he ensured.

Yet he is not an altogether forgotten man in Arizona. The company town near Bisbee bears his name, and in the Mines and Metallurgy building at the University of Arizona there is a bronze plaque which reads:

DEDICATED TO THE MEMORY OF
JAMES DOUGLAS, 1837–1918,
THIS BUILDING IS THE GIFT OF PHELPS DODGE CORPORATION,
OF WHICH HE WAS THE GUIDING SPIRIT FROM 1881 TO 1918.
HE LOVED THE SOUTHWEST AND CONTRIBUTED MIGHTILY
TO ITS DEVELOPMENT.
SCIENTIST AND SCHOLAR, FRIEND OF ARIZONA AND ITS PEOPLE.

Was it because of his Canadian nationality that Dr. Douglas was spurned in favor of a less famous Phelps Dodge engineer, John C. Greenway, developer of the company's New Cornelia mine at Ajo, when Arizona's first representative was chosen for Statuary Hall in Washington? The likelier explanation is that Greenway's widow, Isabelle King Greenway, was then Arizona's first woman in Congress. Dr. Douglas's son James and a grandson Lewis carried on the name in Arizona mining, banking, scholarship, and foreign service.

The big villain of Arizona copper was William Andrews Clark, whose first land of plunder was Montana. Beginning as a frontier storekeeper, Clark climbed over others to found Anaconda Company, that other colossus of copper. His money enabled him to buy what he lusted for. Such was a seat in the United States Senate. Such was the United Verde mine.

Dr. Douglas had scouted the dormant United Verde at Jerome near Prescott for Phelps Dodge, and reported that because of its remoteness from transportation the investment would not prove profitable. He was wrong for perhaps the only time after he reached age fifty.

Whereupon Clark came down from Montana, donned miner's clothes, and with pick and lamp spent two weeks in a close inspection of the mine. He bought and developed it and built his own narrow-gauge railway to connect with the Santa Fe between Prescott and Ashfork. He also built his own company town—Clarkdale, of course.

Before he shut down the United Verde as profitably exhausted, Clark took $72,000,000 out of Arizona. Neither in Montana nor in Arizona did he leave any monument other than a bad name. His art collection went to the Corcoran Gallery in Washington. His bookish son Junior gave memorial libraries to the University of Nevada and UCLA and a law school to the University of Virginia.

The often overlooked beneficial uses of copper in the nation's economy are myriad, and the effects of its production on Arizona's standard of living are apparent to this day in such basics as roads and schools.

No one can deny the awesome sight of the now defunct Lavender Pit at Bisbee and of the other still-working open-pit mines at Morenci and Ajo around whose terraces the machines crawl like ravenous bugs. Even the mauve-colored slag heap at Ajo is lovely to look upon. If one can overlook what the smoke, even when "scrubbed," does to vegetation and to respiratory tracts, then the creamy flow from the high stacks is of towering beauty. The often poor visibility in central and southern Arizona is mistakenly blamed on the smelters when it is more often from dust than smoke.

When we come to balance the good and bad effects of copper in Arizona, it is true that the former are far greater. The state owes more to copper than to any other single factor. Without the support of copper's appointees on the Board of Regents, notably Samuel Morris, the university would not have developed as it has. Copper's benefits have so permeated the state that they are now taken for granted. And yet no philanthropic figure distinguishes Arizona copper in the way the endowed benefactions of Rockefeller, Carnegie, Frick, Folger, Mellon, Morgan, and Huntington lent their founders lasting memory. *Richesse oblige.*

If we depended upon the entertainment media for our knowledge, we would believe that cattle are as native to Arizona as the other Big C—copper. Not so. Cattle came first with the Spaniards to Mexico in 1521 and to Arizona two decades later with Coronado.[14] The wiry Andalusian breed was as well suited to the arid Southwest as the Spaniards themselves. One has only to see the sunbaked provinces of Spain to understand why their natives named Mexico and the Southwest *Nueva España*—New Spain. The Southwest's extremes of heat and cold, scarcity of water, and turquoise skies resembled the mother country's.

Likewise, the little Andalusian cattle were at home in New Spain. The Coronado expedition set out with a herd of them, most of which were abandoned in Sinaloa to run wild when they proved a drag on progress. It is unlikely that any of the survivors of this first *entrada* were the ancestors of the breed in southern Arizona. Indians probably ate them.

More than a century passed before Spaniards came this way again, although they were in the north at the Hopi mesas in the latter 16th century. Then it was Kino who brought cattle to Pimería Alta. Ever since his time they have been a part of the landscape and the economy. Horses and sheep also came with the missionaries. The Apaches welcomed these livestock as enrichments of their own lean economy and rapidly embraced new modes of raiding into Mexico.

By the time Cooke's wagon train came through, the only Mexican cattle that had not been butchered for beef by the Apaches were a few bands of wild cattle. These did not fear to

14. Jay J. Wagoner, *History of the Cattle Industry in Southern Arizona, 1540–1940,* University of Arizona, Social Science Bulletin 20 (Tucson, Arizona, 1952).

attack the train as it reached the San Pedro, and on December 11, 1846, there occurred the brisk engagement which Cooke many years later humorously described as "the Battle of Bull Run."

Although some cattle were raised by the American settlers during the 1850s and 1860s, the Apache threat prevented any large endeavors. Few had the staying power of Pete Kitchen, whose spread on the Santa Cruz was constantly threatened by the Indians. It was sardonically referred to by him as the route of "Tucson, Tubac, Tumacácori, to Hell."

Not until the Apaches were "Crook'd" did animal husbandry become profitable. The land of southeastern Arizona was a cattleman's dream of grass. Grama and sacaton flourished in the rainy seasons of winter and summer. Like the Santa Cruz, the San Pedro was a perennial stream, thickly wooded and bordered with grass. Overgrazing and subsequent erosion lay in the future.

By the mid-1870s the ranges had been heavily stocked with Mexican and Texan cattle and the grasses cropped to the roots. In the next two decades rivulets became deep gullies and then wide arroyos. Along the San Pedro the invading mesquite established itself in thickets that persist to this day from Benson to Redington and beyond. Burning the riverbank brush to drive out the wild cattle only resulted in more erosion. Conservation was unknown.

Great herds were driven in from Texas and Sonora to supply the army and the reservation Indians with beef in a trade-off as they stopped hunting and raiding and became sedentary agriculturists and later stockmen themselves. Southeast of Tucson around Sonoita and Patagonia, English interests founded the Vail and Empire spreads, while farther east Colonel Henry C. Hooker's Sierra Bonita ranch filled the entire Sulphur Spring Valley.

Hooker was a man who lent himself to a blend of history, folklore, and literature, a kind of hero of the range. His beginnings were unlikely. His first stake, it is said, came from the

Paul Bunyanesque feat of shooing a flock of five hundred turkeys over the Sierra Nevada from California to the silver mines, where he cleaned up by selling them for a fat price to the hungry miners of Nevada.

Then in Texas he turned his stake into a herd of shorthorns, which he drove to Arizona and sold to emigrants on the Gila Trail. When he saw the rich rangeland extending from Fort Grant at the foot of the Pinaleños to the border Chiricahuas, he went no farther. Claim after claim he filed until the valley was his.

That it lay athwart the domain of Cochise, war chief of the Chiricahua Apaches, would have daunted a lesser man. Recognizing the stomach as a basic organ, Hooker filled the Apaches' with fresh beef. He is also said to have had woven a great blanket which bore the name of his friend Cochise. It proved so cherished by the chief that he made it his burial blanket.

The Sierra Bonita became the most celebrated ranch in all of Arizona, famed no more for its size and wealth than for its hospitality. It and its owner live in literature as the subjects of *Arizona,* Augustus Thomas's turn-of-the-century stage success, and of *Arizona Nights,* a book of stories by Stewart Edward White. White had come to the Sierra Bonita as a honeymoon guest. Hooker apparently resented the literary license taken by the young writer and threatened to sue him, whereupon White "let him have it" in a brutal sequel called *The Killer.*

Like the others who found in Arizona's resources exportable riches, Hooker went elsewhere for a life of elegance. In his case, as in that of William Andrews Clark, Jr., it was to West Adams Boulevard, the millionaires' row of Los Angeles. He became a well-known traveler on the Southern Pacific. Boarding the Sunset Limited once at Willcox without cash in his pocket, folklore has it, Hooker said to the conductor, "I'm Hooker, charge it." Whereupon the woman across the aisle spoke up. "I'm a hooker too," she said. "Can I charge my fare?"

The coming of the east-west railroads in the early 1880s—the Atlantic and Pacific, which became the Santa Fe in the north, and the Southern Pacific down Mexico way—completed the thrust of rails from coast to coast. Trappers and explorers, wagon traders, soldiers and surveyors, gold rushers, the Pony Express and the Butterfield Overland Mail (St. Louis to San Francisco via Tucson in 23 days)—these consolidated the southern corridor through Arizona.

The corruption of public officials by railroad interests was as prevalent in Arizona as it was in California. The biggest of the Big Four, Collis P. Huntington (uncle of Henry E. of library fame), once wrote to an Arizona legislator, "Can you have Safford call the legislature together and grant such charters as we want at a cost of $25,000? [15] When it took only part of the money to turn the trick, the balance was returned to Huntington with the explanation that Arizonans came cheaper than the magnate had estimated.

Copper, cattle, and lumbering inevitably flourished from the markets opened by the completed rail lines and the several north-south feeder systems. There was also conflict as the railroads exploited their monopoly. At one time the cattlemen of southern Arizona revolted against the rising rates and trail-drove their herds to the Pacific market.

Throughout the territorial decades individual merchants and traders carried on the lucrative business of supplying miners and stockmen, soldiers and docile Indians with food and goods. And in doing so there were laid the foundations of family fortunes, some of which endure to this day, including Ochoa, Steinfeld, Zeckendorf, Levy, and Jácome in the south, the Goldwaters in the Prescott area, and the Babbitts in the north.

The latter is the most celebrated trading dynasty in Arizona's history, originating in the 1880s when five brothers from Ohio began in Flagstaff with a general store and parlayed it into an empire of stores and mills, trading posts, lumberyards, banks and cattle ranches and—in our day—supermarkets throughout the northern towns and on the reservation.

---

15. Lamar, *The Far West,* p. 463.

Thanks to the Spaniards' lack of protective measures, the enterprising Navajos became the first Arizona sheepherders. Their lands were soon overgrazed. When large-scale Anglo sheepherding began in the north, there was some conflict with the cattlemen. This led Zane Grey to write his popular (and misleading) novel of the Graham-Tewksbury feud in the Tonto Basin called *To the Last Man*. The truth is that on the largest spreads in northern Arizona, especially the Babbitts', sheep and cattle ranged together.

If the nineteenth century brought few permanent settlers, the reasons were obvious: the harsh nature of the land and the Apache resistance. Life was often too hard and dangerous for those who wanted to settle and work and make a new life in a new land. Yet there were always those pioneers willing to endure heat and thirst and Indian threats to win homes for themselves in an unpromising setting.

There were the Mormons who came down from Utah, over the Colorado at the Crossing of the Fathers, and took up farms and planted Lombardy poplars for their towering beauty if not for their shade. Their settlements endure to this day: at St. Johns on the Little Colorado, at St. David on the San Pedro and Safford on the Gila, at Snowflake and Showlow on the Mogollon Plateau, and at Mesa in the Salt River Valley, where their temple and gardens make an oasis. The strong blood of the Mormons bred the clan of Udall whose scions, Stewart and Morris, became the peers of Barry Goldwater as public servants on the national scene.

Though always a minority, the Mormons by their industry and integrity have played major roles in Arizona's development. Of the greatest significance, perhaps, is their devotion to the land in a symbiotic relationship akin to that which existed between the Indians and Arizona before it was disrupted. If all Arizonans had emulated the Mormons and planted trees wherever they went, it would now be a more gracious land.

5

The Forty-Eighth Star

TATEHOOD came the hard way. The entry of Arizona and New Mexico in 1912 ended the longest admission struggle in the nation's history. For more than half a century the two aspirants endured their second-class status. In the eyes of Washington the Southwest was a desert in the thrall of Indians and Mexicans, among which a handful of heroic Americans was perilously engaged in mining and ranching.

The coming of the railroads accelerated the struggle between proponents and opponents of statehood. By 1890 the former had gained the momentum that would probably have achieved success for both territories by the turn of the century if new national issues had not appeared. These created turbulence in which the remote territories were tossed about and which postponed their destinies for another two decades.

By 1900 the country was involved in three great debates that had a crippling effect upon the aspirations of Arizona and New Mexico. The first was the aftermath of the war with Spain, which made Hispanic New Mexico a dubious addition to the states of the Union. The second was the cause of conservation and a new awareness of the Southwest's resources of land, forests, and water. The third was the rise of those political-reform movements known as progressivism, which gave power to the people in the form of the initiative, referendum, and recall.

In all of these controversies President Theodore Roosevelt was involved, as an imperialistic nationalist who led the Rough Riders in Cuba, as a spokesman for conservation, and as a champion of reform. Inasmuch as his mounted volunteers were recruited mostly from the Southwest and his own outlook was passionately Western, Roosevelt would seem to have been a leader in the territories' drive for statehood. Such was not the case. For political and conservation reasons he remained passive. Admission did not occur until he had been succeeded by President William Howard Taft.

One villain in the fight—to continue my rather simplistic view of Arizona's history—was Senator Albert Beveridge of Indiana, the chairman of the Committee on Territories. When an omnibus bill was introduced in 1902 to admit Arizona, New Mexico, and Oklahoma as separate states, Beveridge favored "American" Oklahoma, but not "Spanish" New Mexico nor "Frontier" Arizona. When he led his committee to the Southwest on a tour of inspection, the senators moved so fast that proponents of the bill complained of being unable to catch up to present their argument.

In a speech before the House of Representatives after the Beveridge visit, Marcus Aurelius Smith, Arizona's longtime Territorial Delegate (who preferred to be called Mark) said, "I met the committee—I never could have overtaken it—at Phoenix, and it remained there one day, the longest stop in all its record as far as I know, and 'investigated' a police judge and some census enumerators, and had an interpreter with them scouring the town to see whether some Mexicans could not be found who could not speak English, and thus prove valuable witnesses for the purpose of the investigation." [1]

Chairman Beveridge was suspicious of those who spoke

---

1. Bernard L. Fontana, "The 48th Star," *Tucson Daily Citizen,* Semi-Centennial edition, 14 February 1962.

Spanish, viewing adherence to their language as a form of trea-
son. The Mormons in Arizona were also seen by him as potential traitors. As an ardent progressive and enemy of senators
who had interests in the West, Beveridge saw the mining and
railroad interests as combining to gain control of Arizona—as
indeed they were to do. Quality of people, not quantity of land,
he declared, should be the primary criterion for admission. Arizona, he concluded, was no more than a mining camp. He
favored admitting only Indian Oklahoma, and accordingly in
1907 it became the forty-sixth state.

Then Beveridge proposed an odd subterfuge whereby New
Mexico and Arizona would be admitted as one state to be called
Arizona the Great with its capital in Santa Fe. A howl went up
from Anglo Protestant Arizona when it saw the power going to
more populous Hispanic Catholic New Mexico, which was then
dominantly Republican. When Roosevelt championed this jointure measure, Phoenix promptly changed the name of Roosevelt
Street to Cleveland Street.

The Beveridge resolution was also attacked by Delegate
Smith who said of Beveridge that "he proceeds from his own
argument that one rotten egg is bad, but two rotten ones would
make a fine omelet." [2] Much congressional maneuvering occurred, while Roosevelt attempted to pressure the governors of
the two territories to accept joint admission. They resisted his
efforts.

Mark Smith proved the shrewder strategist, employing the
new populist referendum. He drafted an amendment that allowed the territories to hold a referendum on jointure. If either
failed to approve, the measure would be dead. Although New
Mexico strongly approved, Arizona overwhelmingly voted it
down. Once again progress came to a halt.

Yet the pressure from the two territories was irresistible; on
January 6, 1912, President Taft signed a bill admitting New
Mexico as the forty-seventh state, and soon thereafter on Valen-

2. Lamar, *The Far West*, p. 493.

tine's Day, February 14, 1912, Arizona came in as the forty-eighth. There was rejoicing by flagmakers.

In anticipation of success Arizona had elected a full slate of Democrats as its first state officials. Mark Smith became one of the senators and served continuously until defeated in 1921, adding nine senatorial years to his sixteen as delegate. The other senator was Henry Fountain Ashurst, who remained in Congress for twenty-nine years. Arizona's first congressman, Carl Hayden, had an even longer tenure. First as representative and then as senator, he held office for fifty-seven years, more than any other person in the nation's history. As he rose by seniority to chair the powerful Senate Appropriations Committee, Carl Hayden was able to assure Arizona its fair share of federal funds. His great prestige came from the fairness with which he wielded power.

Thus by electing these able legislators Arizona answered Senator Beveridge's charge that the territory was too uncivilized to merit coequality with the other states of the Union. No western state, in fact no state at all, ever had stronger initial representation in Congress.

Although born in a covered wagon on a sheep ranch near Winnemucca, Nevada, Henry Fountain Ashurst was reared in Arizona where his parents homesteaded on the southern slope of Bill Williams Mountain at about the same time that Martha Summerhayes came that way. Ashurst rode the range for six years before the growth of his mind led him to seek schooling and the study of law. "I could throw fifty-six-pound words clear across the Grand Canyon," he recalled of his cowboy years. "As a matter of course I went into politics." [3]

From District Attorney of Coconino County and the practice of law in Prescott, Ashurst rose to the territorial legislature and finally to the United States Senate. Who could have predicted that this rangy man who could fight with either fists or gun would become the Senate's most charming and hyperbolic orator since Clay and Webster? Fondly self-identified as the Silver-

3. Obituary in the *Los Angeles Times,* 1 June 1962.

Tongued Clarion from Coconino County, Ashurst was also the Senate's most resplendent sartorial member. He wore striped pants and cutaway, and his gold-rimmed pince-nez were secured by a black ribbon. His lifelong passion was for words and their meanings. They were both an affectation and a religion with him as he came to share Emerson's belief that "picturesque language is at once a commending certificate; he who employs it is a man in alliance with the truth and God." [4]

From an estimated five thousand speeches made by Ashurst in and out of the Senate, Barry Goldwater early in his own senatorial career chose fourteen that seemed to him to represent the full gamut of Ashurst's genius, and of them he wrote:

> We will find hard common sense; . . . There will be sarcasm of a deep, biting nature, but cast in words that are polite even in their lacerating effect. There are pure orations which are models of polysyllabic effect. There is the after-dinner speech, which of late has fallen to a lowly state. The eulogy . . . the solemn, scholarly thesis . . . the humor . . . and the laughter of the campfire. [5]

I too found myself stirred when I came upon that volume of Ashurst's speeches. No more gracious utterance was ever voiced on the floor of the Senate than his speech of September 11, 1940, conceding defeat. He began in humorous vein, "Coming to the Capitol in a taxicab, the young man who was driving said, 'Senator, what are you going to do for a living now?' I said, 'I think I shall sell apples.' He said, 'What do you mean by that?' I replied, 'Well, for almost thirty years I have successfully distributed apple-sauce in the Capitol. I ought now to be able to sell a few apples.' " [6]

Wickedly barbed was Ashurst's harpooning of the "Kingfish" in his speech of June 15, 1935, holding up to scorn Senator Huey Long of Louisiana. So taken was I by the timeliness of this latter speech that during the time when Senator Joseph Mc-

4. *Speeches of Henry Fountain Ashurst,* edited by Barry Goldwater (Phoenix: Arizona-Messenger Co., 1954), p. viii.

5. *Speeches of Ashurst,* p. x.

6. *Speeches of Ashurst,* pp. 69–70.

Carthy of Wisconsin was outraging many decent Americans, I commissioned a printer to make a bold broadside of that Ashurst speech. Today it hangs on several public walls in Arizona.

In Washington I once called on Senator Ashurst, then living in retirement at the Sheraton Park Hotel. There he showed me his voluminous collection of cartoons of himself, pro and con, collected through his three decades in the Senate. They and his diaries are now preserved at the University of Arizona, and a selection from the latter was published under the title *A Many-Colored Toga.*[7]

My meeting with that pioneer statesman was memorable. Our descent to the dining room became a courtly procession. Everyone encountered deferred to the senator and in return was recognized with smiles, bows, and handshakes, and in the case of an attractive woman, with an embrace. If a babe in arms had been met, it would surely have been kissed. It was a royal antiphonal of respect and response enacted by a natural politician and gracious gentleman.

Arizona's other pioneer senator was that rare figure of his time, a second generation Arizonan, born in Tempe, schooled at the Normal School his father founded, and at Stanford University, then steeled for service in Congress as the sheriff of Maricopa County. Unlike his eloquent colleague from Coconino County, Carl Hayden spoke precisely and factually; and when his state's interests were involved, his vote was ever for Arizona. Although increasingly feeble as he served on into his nineties, Senator Hayden became a symbol of devoted service in American government. From 1912 to 1970 he was the champion and guardian of Arizona in the national arena. Federal expenditures in Arizona during that time are lasting evidence of Carl Hayden's loyalty to his native state. Highways, dams for irrigation, flood control and power, public buildings, Indian benefits, and finally the Central Arizona Project—these instances of fed-

7. *A Many-Colored Toga: The Diary of Henry Fountain Ashurst,* edited by G. F. Sparks (Tucson: University of Arizona Press, 1962).

eral largesse were coincident with his control of the Appropriations Committee. His papers are preserved at Arizona State
University in his home town of Tempe, and the university library there bears his father's honored name.

As varied and notable as were the characters and contributions of these first congressional representatives, Arizona's
dominant political personality for twenty years was the state's
first governor, George Wiley Paul Hunt. Elected to seven terms
in all, in and out of office from 1912 to 1934, Hunt was a traditional up-from-poverty American hero, a fitting successor to, albeit a more practical man than "Father" Poston. His ancestry,
dating from Revolutionary times, and his early tempering on the
frontier, his success as a businessman and his political season-
ing, as well as his ideas, sympathies, and humble way of life,
all formed a personality Arizonan to the core. The name Paul
had always been borne by someone in each generation since the
family's descent from John Paul Jones, our early naval hero.

In George Wiley Paul Hunt were personified the issues and
aspirations of his time, to which he gave blunt voice and effective realization. His identification with the common man and his
idealism enabled him repeatedly to gain and regain public office. He came eventually to regard the governor's chair as his
rightful possession. When after being elected for the fifth time
he was sarcastically hailed as George the Fifth, Hunt un-
abashedly vowed to seek the office again and again—and did so
until he ended as George the Seventh.

George Wiley Paul Hunt was born in Missouri in 1859 and
ran away from an impoverished home at fourteen to seek his
fortune in the West. His was a hard search during which he rode
the rails as a tramp, rousted about in Colorado and New Mexico, prospected for lost mines, and escaped from Indians and
bandits. In this way he came to know the life and lot of common people on the frontier.

In 1881 at the age of 22 the future Democratic monarch of
Arizona trudged into the mining camp of Globe in Gila County.

His companion was a pack burro. Destiny had brought him to his inevitable place. Although as territorial legislator and then as governor Hunt was to spend much time in Phoenix, Globe was ever his stronghold. There he would end his campaign for re-election with a torchlight parade and a rousing speech to his fellow townsmen.

He began as a helper in a general store, the Old Dominion, and rose to be president of the company. He also worked as dishwasher and waiter in the restaurant next door. Frank C. Lockwood tells of a certain man who came to Globe in the early days with a pack train to obtain supplies. Hunt waited on him at the restaurant. When campaigning in the man's hometown years later, Hunt heard that the man had declared, "I won't vote for Hunt; he used to wait on me." Whereupon Hunt sought him out and, according to Lockwood, the following dialogue took place:

"Do you remember me?"
"Yes, I do. You used to wait on me."
"I was a pretty good waiter, wasn't I?"
"Yes."
"Well, I would make just as good a governor." [8]

The issues in the constitutional convention of 1910, held in preparation for statehood and over which Hunt presided, were the controversial issues Hunt was to continue to champion as governor. They included women's suffrage, child-labor laws, school desegregation, the abolition of capital punishment, prevention of juvenile crime, and lessening of corporate control. Some are alive to this day. The record also shows that Hunt was often anti-Mexican and a soak-the-rich opportunist.

The delegates were subjected to vigorous advice from their constituents, particularly on the subject of women's suffrage. Two hundred voters in Bisbee sent the following communication to their representative: "Your supporters in Bisbee are proud of your nerve in the matter of the introduction of the

8. Frank C. Lockwood, *Pioneer Portraits* (Tucson: University of Arizona Press, 1968), p. 210.

Women's Suffrage Proposition. Move up to Apache County and stay there. You are a bum." And from Douglas: "Your constituents of Cochise County thank you not to come back. You ought to be shot." Hunt suggested that such communications be referred to the Committee on Militia and Public Defense.[9]

The suffrage proposal failed to make its way into the constitution when Hunt did not push for it. The women of Arizona had to wait until the regular November election of 1912 before winning the right to vote, and handily did they win, 13,452 to 6,202. Even now in 1976 they have yet to achieve full rights with men.

The makeup of the constitutional convention included fifty-one Democrats and eleven Republicans; fourteen lawyers, nine cattlemen, five miners, four merchants; and the balance ranged from ministers to saloon keepers. Its progressive-populist leanings troubled the Eastern establishment to the extent that President Taft made a trip to Arizona and warned against a "crank constitution." He threatened to veto admission if the provision for recall of judges was left in. Accordingly it was taken out, only to be put back in as soon as Taft had signed the admissions bill. It was the same independent attitude Arizona has always had toward the rest of the country and which in our era has led it to remain the year round on Mountain Standard Time.

George Wiley Paul Hunt did not achieve his repeated success by being a starry-eyed reformer. He was as practical and realistic a politician as Arizona was not to see again until the advent of Barry Goldwater. Whereas Senator Ashurst's defeat in 1940 by his fellow Democrat, Judge Ernest McFarland, was laid to his failure to come home and woo the voters, Hunt never isolated himself in Phoenix. He was away from the capital probably more than he was in it. He was a leader, not a follower. Too often the Arizona legislature was neither. Consider these items recommended in Governor Hunt's first address to the legislature: encouragement of agricultural education, old-age pensions,

9. Fontana, "The 48th Star."

workmen's compensation, anti-usury laws, a merit system for state employees.

Hunt was also a proponent of a statewide network of good roads to be built with prison labor, a position arrived at after a trip to Europe had acquainted him with the Roman roads of France and Britain. It was a position opposed by the railroads who influenced the legislature by the distribution of passes and other emoluments.

The governor was an inveterate traveler by automobile. No hamlet, crossroads, or bridge dedication was too remote for him to visit, make a speech, shake hands, and thus garner votes for re-election. He traveled with a card file beside him on the back seat in which were listed the names and idiosyncrasies of thousands of Arizona voters. Many a vote was his after that voter was recognized and called by name. Simple? Yes—and effective, then and now. Recognition is a basic human need.

As a self-educated man whose grammar and spelling were admittedly imperfect, Hunt championed public education and free textbooks. An interest in prison welfare led him when en route from Phoenix to Globe to break the journey in Florence, where he would spend Saturday night in the warden's guest room in the prison. On Sunday morning any inmate could bring his troubles to the governor. Once when the guards wanted to attend a traveling show, the governor and his aide took over the tower and kept watch on the wall. While the governor was in Phoenix, his door was open to all. No letter went unanswered. He had the common touch that comes only from love of his fellowmen— plus a passion for re-election.

Two labor disputes that drew national attention found Governor Hunt on the side of the miners to the extent that he was denounced by the press as a dangerous radical. These involved strikes at the Phelps Dodge mines in Clifton-Morenci and Bisbee. The latter was the scene of the deportation of I.W.W.-affiliated miners, one of the most stark instances of frontier vigilantism, although generally a popular position in Arizona in 1917.

There was a rough consistency in all that Hunt did. He avoided conflict of interest by selling his holdings in Globe and investing the money in government securities. He met the opposition head on, knowing that his "radicalism" was only good old grass-roots Americanism. "Those who believe in government by privilege rather than government by the people find it easy to use the terms 'IWW' and 'Bolshevik,' " he said, "but my ideas of democracy were formed before these terms came into being, and will remain adamant when the IWW and the Bolshevik shall have gone the way of the mugwumps and the populists." [10] Although most newspapers in the state, save the *Arizona Silver Belt,* were against him, he persisted in being re-elected.

George Wiley Paul Hunt was no carpetbagger, no latecomer seeking spoils from Arizona's riches. He was almost as native as the copper whose absentee owners he flayed, particularly at election time when he presented himself to the voters as a man who had never worn a copper collar. His two basic political slogans were Efficiency and Loyalty, which meant that if the state's jobs were well done and the state's governor unfailingly supported, then Arizona would be well served and its faithful servants rewarded.

An exotic interlude in Hunt's career came in 1920 when, after he was surprisingly pushed out of the governor's chair, he was appointed by President Woodrow Wilson as Envoy Extraordinary and Minister Plenipotentiary to the Kingdom of Siam. There Hunt enjoyed much free time for sight-seeing. He was photographed beside an also massive white elephant. Postcards by the hundreds were mailed back to his former constituents. He might be out of sight, but damned if he would be out of mind; and it was not long after his return that they returned him once again to his favorite chair. He brought back souvenirs of Siam, including native dress in which he sometimes appeared and spoke.

10. Lockwood, *Pioneer Portraits,* p. 206.

Arizona's absentee railroad and mining interests based in San Francisco and New York were not Hunt's only enemies. A greater villain was California, which insisted on taking more than its share of water from the Colorado River. Hunt particularly opposed all Republican-sponsored compacts that limited Arizona's rights to her greatest river. He saw in the plans for building generating dams a plot by the "power trust." He was against such federal invasion of his state's rights, although he knew that federal spending was essential to Arizona's economic well-being.

His advancing age and the Depression finally ended Hunt's reign as the Old Roman, or, as his enemies called him (looking at his egg-bald head, flowing mustache, and girth), the Old Walrus. Like Poston (whose reburial on Primrose Hill was attended by Hunt) the old governor was laid to rest on a hill. He had built his tomb in Papago Park between Phoenix and Tempe. There the white-tile pyramid under which he and his wife came to rest overlooks the Salt River Valley "that in the years to come," Hunt once prophesied, "will be the mecca of those that love beautiful things and in a state where the people rule."

With the long tenure of these first state officials—Smith, Ashurst, Hayden, and Hunt—a continuity was ensured during which Arizona consolidated its position as the forty-eighth state. In the uncertain beginning, such proved the wise course. It also afforded Will Rogers a quip when in 1931 he was present with Governor Hunt at the dedication of Sky Harbor Airport in Phoenix.

"How's your hereditary governorship coming along?" Rogers asked Hunt as Rogers concluded his talk. "If you want to adopt me, I'll come over here and take it off your hands when you get ready." [11] Hunt only smiled. He was old, his mind dulled, and he probably missed the point.

More than any other in Arizona's history, George Wiley Paul

11. John S. Goff, *George W. P. Hunt and His Arizona* (Pasadena: Socio Technical Publications, 1973), p. 122.

Hunt personified the way social progress is achieved—by creating and then neutralizing polarities, and by keeping tensions from snapping. By tilting his power toward Labor, Hunt prevented Capital from excessive exploitation, and by placing the good of the commonwealth above that of the corporation, he won favor for his fairness and courage. Lincolnesque in his simple, earthy ways, some saw him only as crude; he nevertheless gave Arizona lasting character.

"During his long career not a suspicion of crookedness sullied Hunt's reputation," biographer Frank Lockwood wrote.

> His rude, crude strength, his defiance of money and the money interests, his detestation of snobbery and pretension, whether social or intellectual, his bighearted humanity, and his extraordinary intellectual shrewdness and political foresight made him the trusted champion and advocate of the people and the scourge of the unjust, the dishonest, and the autocratic.[12]

Fortunate was Arizona to have had such a man at the helm in its infant years as the "baby" state. George Wiley Paul Hunt was *the* man for those times.

12. Lockwood, *Pioneer Portraits,* p. 235.

6

Taming the Wild Rivers

ILDEST of all was the Colorado. It should have been named the Arizona or the Utah, for its name never came from the Rocky Mountain state. *Colorado* means "red" in Spanish, and that color of its water is due to neither Colorado nor Arizona, but rather to the red earth of Utah, through which it ravenously runs, engorging tons of silt and rock.

The Spaniards gave it various names. Alarcón saw it first in 1539 when sailing upriver from the Gulf; farther north Cárdenas came upon it in 1540 as a result of the scouting expedition on which he was sent by Coronado. Cárdenas wasn't searching for scenery. Gold was his goal. Centuries were to pass before the Grand Canyon of the Colorado proved Arizona's most golden attraction.

The Grand Canyon impressed Cárdenas as no more than a wide gash in the earth. Three of his nimbler men tried to reach the river seen below. They never made it. The climb proved too rough. Their partial descent is believed to have been at the point we call Grand View.

Although it rises in the Rockies far to the northeast of Arizona and starts out like any other river, the Colorado grows to greatness by gathering tributary after tributary—all the rivers, creeks, and streams of the western slope of the Rockies, so that by the time it reaches Arizona, the Colorado is a savage river, biting ever deeper into the body of earth, eating out the grandest of all river canyons.

Water alone is not responsible; the power comes from the grinding action of the river's tonnage of silt and rock. By their very size the figures lose meaning—flow of water in second feet, and volume of earth borne by it. For those who want them, the figures are there.

Not until little more than a century ago was the Colorado fully explored. The complex of canyons up near the source long remained unmapped. Futile efforts had been made to go downstream by boat. While en route to disaster in Death Valley, a party of gold seekers tried to take the easy way by river. Their boat was smashed in a rapids, and they barely escaped with their lives. A *voyageur* by the name of D. (for Denis) Julien was determined to be remembered. During 1836 he carved his name on the canyon walls at six different places. The last was in Cataract Canyon at a stretch of smooth water above rapids and at a height that would have been possible only if he had been in a boat at high water. Thereafter Monsieur Julien disappears from history. It is likely that the rapids engulfed him and his craft.

Who else tried it? James White probably made it in 1867. He was a prospector who took to the river to escape from the Indians.[1] Perhaps some aborigine set forth on his raft of cottonwood logs and was swept all the way downriver? We'll never know. Those early ones only lived their history. There was no one to write it, no language to write it in.

Powell is honored as the first to make it through, and with him—Major John Wesley Powell—began the sequence of events that led to our watered and powered Arizona. If I were a genealogy buff, I would have wasted my time seeking in vain to link with his lineage, for he is the greatest of the Powells.

He was a man magnetized by that unmapped heartland of the

1. R. E. Lingenfelter, *First Through the Grand Canyon* (Los Angeles: Glen Dawson, 1958) a summary of the evidence in favor of White.

Rockies. Was he therefore an adventurer, a treasure hunter, a land claimer? None of these. He was just plain curious, a man moved by the same scientific curiosity that takes men to the moon and eventually to the planets.

Powell began as an Illinois college professor of geology. He is said to have led the first student field trips. Their destination was the remote uplands of the Rocky Mountains, where they explored the headwaters of the Colorado. Powell had grown up on the prairies and waterways of the Mississippi Valley where he had learned to cope with wilderness and to handle small boats. While serving the North in the Civil War, he lost his right arm at Shiloh. His later feats of strength, agility, and endurance in running the river and scaling its cliffs were the more remarkable for having been done with only one arm. Few could have matched him with a dozen. He had a kind of humorous sense, as revealed in his writing to a fellow officer who had lost his left arm, suggesting that henceforth they buy and share a single pair of gloves.

Major Powell was curious, determined, courageous, and able, a planner and organizer. All of these qualities were needed to carry him through the perilous adventure to his fame. During twenty also perilous years in Washington, he created bureaus of Geology and Ethnology and laid the groundwork for the Bureau of Reclamation and the taming of the wild rivers. Powell was of the same breed as Kino and Anza. His work in field and Capital has meaning today far beyond his name on the lake at Glen Canyon.

Powell's published accounts of the two river runs made by him and his men form a classic of Southwest literature. Less dramatic but of more lasting significance is his *Report on the Lands of the Arid Regions of the United States,* which appeared in 1878. It is a far-reaching work that led to the west of dams, flood control, irrigation, and power generation, to national parks and forests and federal management of the arid lands.

We can read this epochal work in a reprint introduced by Wallace Stegner, the inspired biographer of Powell:

It is the classic statement of the terms on which the West could be peopled . . . it forecasts with disconcerting accuracy the droughts, floods, crop failures, land and water monopolies, jurisdictional quarrels, and individual tragedies which have been the consequences of applying wet-country habits in a dry country.
. . . In the West, which characteristically has not been so much settled as raided—first for its furs, then for its minerals, then for its grass, then in some places for its timber, in some for its wheat, on some for its scenery—consequences have habitually been ignored.[2]

Although Theodore Roosevelt failed to champion Arizona's claim to statehood until a few days before he left the presidency, he proved himself otherwise one of its best friends. From his experience as a rancher and hunter in the Dakota Badlands he came to know the west's extremes of heat and cold, of drought and flood. He saw the logic of Powell's thesis that the arid lands make their own laws and that in their domain the key to life and death is water. He who owned the water owned all.

As Powell lay dying in 1902, word was brought that President Roosevelt was pushing through the legislation to create the Bureau of Reclamation: "It is as right for the national government," Roosevelt declared, "to make the streams and rivers of the arid region useful by engineering works for water storage as to make useful the rivers and harbors of the humid region by engineering works of another kind." Powell was deeply moved by the news. "These things take time," he said to his informant. "You must learn to control impatience, but always be impatient." [3]

The founding of the Bureau of Reclamation led to the first successful effort to tame the Colorado and to the Arizona we know today. It came on the lower river where the threat of re-

2. John Wesley Powell, *Report on the Arid Lands,* edited by Wallace Stegner (Cambridge, Mass., Belknap Press, 1962), p. xxiv.
3. Lawrence C. Powell, *Southwest Classics* (Los Angeles: Ward Ritchie Press, 1974), p. 292.

current disaster made action imperative. In the spring of 1906 the river again broke through its bank at flood stage and poured across the Imperial Valley to the lowest point below sea level, where it re-formed California's ancient Salton Sea to a size which remains to this day a large body of water. If the river had not been finally contained through massive rock dumping by the Southern Pacific (villain into hero!) the entire valley, which produces a large part of the nation's fresh vegetables, would be under water.

Accordingly Laguna Dam, an Indian weir-type barrier, was thrown across the river sixteen miles above Yuma. The immediate beneficiary was California on the lower side of the river. The All-American Canal (so-called because it was dug on the American side of the Mexican border) took the Colorado's docile water and by gravity flow spread it over the Imperial Valley to the profit of farmers and consumers.

The Bureau of Reclamation did not play favorites among the arid states. After the benefit to California from Laguna came an even greater dam to control Arizona's other wild rivers, the Salt and the lower Gila into which the Salt flows. High in the mountains northeast of Phoenix a masonry dam was built in the narrow canyon below the confluence of Tonto Creek and the Salt, creating a lake that backed up water more than twenty miles into the Tonto Basin.

This was the greatest dam yet to be built in the country, and it remains the largest masonry dam in the world. Engineered by Louis C. Hill, it was made from materials on the site—of sandstone blocks quarried from the canyon's sides and bonded with local cement. Electrical power was generated by the diverted river. Supplies were hauled in by mule teams from Mesa over a sixty-mile road blasted from the rock walls of the Salt River and adjoining canyons. Much of the labor was done by Tonto Apaches.

The name of Theodore Roosevelt was given to the dam and the lake, and on March 18, 1911, nine years after he had signed the Reclamation Act making such works possible, President

Roosevelt dedicated the massive structure. He gave a memorable speech. Although I have no evidence at hand, my belief is that T.R. might have been the last of our presidents to write his own speeches. More than a politician, he was a maker of history and literature and one of our few presidents we can call heroic.

His concluding words on that day of dedication were simple and moving. "I do not know if it is of any consequence to a man," he said, "whether he has a statue after he is dead. If there could be any monument which could appeal to any man, surely it is this. You could not have done anything which would have pleased and touched me more than to name this great dam, this great reservoir site after me, and I thank you from my heart for having done so." [4]

It was simply Roosevelt Dam for more than forty-five years. After the death of Franklin Delano Roosevelt, a growing phalanx of detractors feared newcomers might think the dam was meant to honor F.D.R., so its name was changed by Congress to Theodore Roosevelt Dam.

Now, many years after my Washington childhood when on Sunday mornings President Roosevelt would ride by on his white horse and wave to us children in front of our terraced houses along Park Road, I have gone to that dam on the Salt, even as I have returned to Laguna on the Colorado, and stood there overlooking lake and canyon and paid homage to those whose vision made our world. The heroism of Major Powell and President Roosevelt determined our destiny as Arizonans. If you would seek the evidence, take the dusty road from Apache Junction to the great rock dam on the Salt. It will be there till Judgment Day.

These and later dams in the Southwest had three aims: to control flooding, to impound water for irrigation, and to generate electricity. Because of its snowy origins and vast drainage area, the Colorado never runs dry. This is not true of the Gila. Except

4. Full text of speech in *Arizona Highways* 36:4 (April 1961) 32–33.

in time of flood when it runs as wild as any, the Gila flows along mostly out of sight, an odd kind of upside-down river. Farmers along its course have been hurt more by drought than by flood.

Thus the intention of the next great reclamation project in Arizona was to dam the Gila and create a storage lake from which the farmers below could draw water in times of drought. The site was at the head of a canyon that cuts through the Pinals to free the river on its final run past Florence, the town of Coolidge, and Gila Bend to the Colorado at Yuma.

The site provoked controversy when it appeared that the impounded water would inundate Apache lands, including hundreds of wickiups as well as the camp from which Geronimo set out on his raids and the sacred burial ground of the San Carlos tribe. Proponents sought to meet the Indians' argument on the latter point by falsely claiming that deceased Apaches were traditionally burned, not buried.

Regardless of protests, the dam was built and San Carlos Lake eventually formed, although at the time of dedication in 1930 by former President Calvin Coolidge, whose name was given to the dam, the lake was mostly dry and grass-grown. In lieu of a moving speech to match Roosevelt's of an earlier time, Will Rogers, the prince of quipsters, remarked to Coolidge, "If this was my lake, I'd mow it." [5]

This dam too has drawn me by the loneliness of its setting, there in an immensity of desert and mountains, and by the fact that it is the domain of Ross Santee, laureate in pictures and prose of Arizona's rangeland. If one would visit Coolidge Dam and Lake San Carlos, he should go in early summer before the heat becomes unbearable. On the rocky slopes of the Pinals the sotol will be in golden flower. And there will be few or no people. It is Arizona's loneliest dam site.

Floods on the Gila still ravage the lands above Coolidge

5. Edward H. Peplow, Jr., *History of Arizona*, 3 vols. (New York: Lewis Publishing Co., 1958), 3:312–313.

Dam. As late as 1973 the valley at Safford, a hundred miles upriver, was underwater to the width of a mile. A wretched shack-town was washed out.

Although *River of the Sun,* Ross Calvin's book about the Gila, appeared thirty years ago, Calvin's words timelessly pose the problem of flood control:

> Myriads of mountain gullies, lowering their level of discharge, gained thus on every hillside an increasing momentum in their attack on the soil; the fertile layer on its surface, which contained most of the plant food, was washed away or else impoverished by the leaching of its nitrogen; the axis of the channel kept swinging year by year so that the river bit out a farm first from one bank and then from the other. The farms were redistributed piecemeal along the riverbed, but most of them were superimposed like layers of a cake behind the Coolidge Dam, precisely where they do the greatest possible harm.[6]

The great dams built later on the Colorado—Hoover and Glen Canyon—are primarily for the generation of electrical power. The chief beneficiary, as it is of the water carried for hundreds of miles by aqueducts, is Greater Los Angeles. California's claim to the water and power is based on the argument that the greatest number of people and industries creates the demand and thereby justifies the need. Economic and political power have supported the claim of the insatiable giant. Arrayed against its might was the small population of Arizona, led by doughty Governor Hunt. As Arizona argued that its need was greater than that of an impoverished tribe of San Carlos Apaches, so did Southern California justify taking the water to the full extent of its needs. All Arizona could do was to carry its fight to the courts. There it proved more successful than when Governor Moeur, Hunt's successor, ordered its National Guard to the riverbank in a vain attempt to halt construction of Parker Dam.

Dammed rivers are changed rivers. Hoover Dam has had a profound effect on the stream below. No longer do silt and rock

6. Ross Calvin, *River of the Sun: Stories of the Storied Gila* (Albuquerque: University of New Mexico Press, 1946), p. 151.

scour the bed clean. Instead they build up behind Glen Canyon Dam in Lake Powell. Someday in the far future all dams will be overwhelmed by rising water, and then the wild river will once again run free to the Gulf.

Today below Hoover Dam the languid river makes bankside marshes of lazy overflow. Nearly a hundred million dollars have been spent in dredging the channel and stabilizing the marshes. The cost will continue. Placid as a canal the tamed river now makes its way to the mouth, which also has been changed. The delta is no longer a network of shifting channels. It is too soon to know what the ultimate effects of the dams will be on the wildlife of the lower river. We do know that the eco-system has been altered. All we can be sure of is that life will continue as it adapts to the new conditions.

Today the lower Colorado is a playground for campers, fishers, and boaters. Dwellers in mobile homes line the banks in an attenuated "catfish culture." At Lake Havasu stands the incongruous reconstruction of London Bridge, one of the most absurd and profitable real-estate gimmicks of our era.

Looking back on a lifetime spent on and near the river during which he wrote the definitive work on the Colorado's delta, the hydrographer Godfrey Sykes wrote these nostalgic words:

> Of course, as an engineer, I fully appreciate the magnificent structures that have brought the lower Colorado under control, and the breadth of their conceptions and planning that made their erection possible, but I must confess that I have much the same sympathy for my old friend, the sometimes wayward, but always interesting, and still unconquered and untrammeled river of the last and preceding centuries, that I have for a bird in a cage, or an animal in a zoo.[7]

Now as more dams are planned between those at Boulder and Glen canyons, as well as the coal-fired plants already on the Colorado and the San Juan which will bring more power (and less water) to California and Arizona, the struggle transcends

7. Godfrey Sykes, *A Westerly Trend* (Tucson: Arizona Pioneers Historical Society, 1944), pp. 312–313.

the old one between the two states. The wider Southwest is now involved. Arizona itself is no longer in agreement on the Central Arizona Project, the dream of Senator Carl Hayden to lift Colorado River water to the lands around Phoenix and even higher to Tucson. Hayden died before his billion-dollar plan was fully funded. There are those in Tucson who distrust Phoenix and the Salt River Valley as all of Arizona once feared Los Angeles and Southern California. Once again "bad water" is rising. The mountainous sources of the Colorado River have new demands on them by the plan to strip-mine the high country.

In the forefront of environmental research is the University of Arizona's Office of Arid Lands Studies. Founded in 1964 under the direction of the distinguished botanist Dr. William G. McGinnies, it has sponsored research conferences and papers and published monumental volumes on the arid lands of Arizona and other places in the world.

Of immediate pertinency to the water needs of the new mining developments is a resource information paper by Charles Bowden, assisted by Patricia Paylore, published in 1975 on "The Impact of Energy Development on Water Resources in the Arid Lands." Its conclusions are cast in laconic terms:

> Many of the consequences of extracting energy from arid lands are not known. But a few are. Arid lands are characterized by a lack of moisture. Energy-conversion systems are characterized by large appetites for water. They will cut into the limited water supply of arid lands. Arid lands are slow to heal from injury. Energy-extraction methods are quick to scar. The energy industry will leave its mark on arid lands.
>
> The drylands are inhospitable to humans and their habits. They will not lose their paucity of water because humans want more water, nor will they lose their fragility because human ways are hard. Whether energy systems now little used or as yet unknown will prove more attuned to the conditions of arid lands is a matter of speculation, not knowledge.
>
> Global societies are eyeing the arid lands because societies are full of appetites and the parched regions are the most vacant on the planet. Available evidence suggests that they are vacant because they are hostile to human ways of life and frequently fail to sustain

such ways. Whether energy-extraction industries will overcome this hostility is a question for which we have only begun to look for an answer.[8]

There is in Arizona a classic demonstration of what water can do when it is led to flow into the right dry place. I mean the phoenix that rose in the desert, the City of Phoenix, capital of the Salt River's Valley of the Sun and of all Arizona.

8. Charles Bowden, "The Impact of Energy Development on Water Resources in the Arid Lands," a Resource Information Paper (Tucson: University of Arizona Office of Arid Lands Studies, 1975), p. 102.

7

Phoenix in the Desert

ACCORDING to Herodotus, the father of history, the phoenix was a mythological bird of the Arabian desert that, after living for centuries, burnt itself on a funeral pyre, then rose from the ashes to live again through a new cycle of time.

When we know that Arizona's Phoenix, now the metropolitan abode of a million souls, rose from the desert on the site of the vanished Hohokam, we realize the aptness of its name. If we embrace the Egyptologist Sir Flinders Petrie's cyclic view of history, then do we wonder how many centuries time has allotted this fair city before its funeral pyre is ready. And beyond that fiery day, what even more miraculous bird will arise from its ashes?

If the ghosts of the Hohokam wander the canyons of the towering city and see that it all depends upon the elements they depended on, they will not be astonished. They did what the Phoenicians have done to exist on the desert; they took the water of the Salt River to sustain their life. There in the Valley of the Sun they lived for their allotted centuries. Then when the exhausted earth would no longer keep them, they went downriver, and their canals were sand-filled and forgotten. Or was it drought or was it war that doomed them? No one knows for sure.

Thus the centuries passed while the river kept its own calendar—flowing, flooding and running dry, as the mountains drained the clouds of their moisture. Water, sun, and soil—the essential elements were there. All that was needed was another race of men for the phoenix to arise not from its ashes but from the rejuvenated river lands.

Then came the Anglos' turn to rule the valley. Indians, Spaniards, and Mexicans had taken theirs. The Salt River Valley was not the most obvious place for a resurrection. Arizona's mother settlement of Tucson lay south of the Gila, her new capital to the northwest, where Prescott's mineral wealth augured growth.

Yet in prehistoric times the center of population had been the valleys of the Salt and the Gila, and for the same reasons that they are today the regions where most Arizonans live: rich alluvial land, a constant water supply that can be easily canalled onto level acreage, abundant sunshine, and mild winters.

The time was 1868 in the fifth year of the territory. The major army forts were in the center—Whipple at Prescott and McDowell on the Verde near its junction with the Salt, located there to keep a gun on the Tonto Apaches. Although the valley of the Salt could serve for agricultural development, it was not then a place to attract many people as residents. Its scenic attractions were nil: a fickle riverbed, a desert of creosote, cactus, and runty mesquite, and a few barren ranges, more hill than mountain. Also scant rainfall and windblown sand and a summer sun that baked the valley in furnace heat. There was no one there, its first inhabitants had long since gone and been forgotten.

How did it happen that the phoenix arose there? Who waved the wand? How pleasing to civic pride if Phoenix could claim a founder as selfless as Kino, as brave as Anza! Alas, its founder was John W. (Jack) Swilling, a tricky adventurer willing to serve whoever paid him the most, Confederate or Union. He was also an Indian hunter and highwayman who came to a sad end in jail at Yuma. No wonder the statue in front of the capitol is that of Lieutenant Frank Luke, Jr., that daring young flyer of World War I instead of Swilling's.

Swilling was a South Carolinian who came to Arizona in 1857 as a hand on a government party to improve the Gila Trail. He then joined a gold rush to Gila City and led a militia party called the Gila Rangers to chastise raiding Yavapais. Lust for gold led him back to the domain of Mangas Coloradas at Piños Altos. It was he who treacherously delivered the Mimbreño chieftain to the Union troops to be murdered. Next we meet Swilling prospecting for gold near Prescott. After squandering the profits of a rich strike, he drifted down to the Salt River Valley and became a hauler of hay to the post at Fort Mc-Dowell. It was a dangerous job, the last three haulers having been killed by the Tontos.

This man was aware of the land's lay and the wind's direction. He saw that the ancient farmers had canalled water to the drier reaches. Vestiges of their ditches were still visible. Swilling knew naught of the Hohokam. He knew only what he needed to know: that when watered, the sun-baked soil would yield crops; and furthermore that the United States Army paid cash for barley and would provide a market for other crops.

And so there at the crossing of the Salt where Phoenix and Tempe now meet and merge, the enterprising adventurer, together with Henry Wickenburg and others, grandly inaugurated the Swilling Irrigating Canal Company. Following the Indians' example, the company dug a ditch north and west from what is today 44th and Washington streets. Along it settled thirty farmers. They soon grew to a hundred, and by 1872 they had increased sevenfold.

As Swilling prospered, he took to wife a Mexican girl, one Trinidad of Tucson, and at what is today the east end of the parking lot at Greyhound Park he built an adobe house. With his wife's aid he enrolled the neighboring Mexicans to vote in newly organized Maricopa County's election to locate the county seat. Their vote was for the site to be centered at Swilling's home and the farming settlement now included in the site of the state hospital. Alas, a rival group of real estate developers paid more for the Indian vote, and so the seat was set where it is today, in downtown Phoenix, west of the original settlement.

This setback plus a native restlessness led Swilling to take up land along the Agua Fria in Black Canyon country up toward Prescott. His career had peaked. From then on his way ran downriver. Because of pain from a head injury suffered in a fight before coming to Arizona, Swilling had become addicted to laudanum and alcohol, neither of which improved his character. He moved outside the law. His fall from grace came with his indictment for the holdup of the Wickenburg stage. Although friends joined in his protest of innocence, circumstantial evidence damned him. He was being held in the Yuma jail awaiting trial when he died in 1878 at the age of forty-eight.

In a last letter he penned these true words: "I will be remembered long after the names of my persecutors have been forgotten." [1]

Now, a century later, Phoenix along with the rest of Arizona is civilized, or at least what we call civilized. Pride in her pioneers grows higher as they recede in history. In this mood of nostalgic reverence, the quixotic failure and treacherous violence of those two early ones are overlooked or forgotten. And yet they are among the founders to be honored at least for their visionary persistence: Poston there at Lincoln's shoulder with ready pen, Swilling with plow and mule, digging the *zanja madre,* the mother ditch.

The naming of Phoenix is owed to yet another eccentric Arizonan, an English wanderer born in France, where his father was in the diplomatic service. With a ready assist from himself, custom conferred upon him no less than a lordship. He was, in fact, descended from the minor nobility, born Bryan Philip Darrel Duppa of Hollingbourne House, County Kent. His early years remain shrouded. They apparently included classical schooling in France and Spain and fluency in the continental languages. Later he suffered shipwreck, explored South

1. Edward Peplow, editor, *The Taming of the Salt* (Phoenix: Salt River Project, 1970), p. 16.

America, and then joined his prosperous Uncle George in developing a sheep station at St. Leonards, New Zealand, where in time he accumulated his own flock and property.

Duppa next appeared in Prescott, N.M.T., in 1862 where he is said to have come to investigate some mining shares owned by his uncle. While prospecting and Indian fighting, he managed to receive via the Bank of California remittances from New Zealand from the sale of his sheep. It was enough to keep him in beans and beer.

Then in 1867 those two oddballs, D. Duppa and J. Swilling, rolled together, we know not how. Was the Englishman the "angel" who staked the Carolinian in that venture on the Salt? We only know Duppa turned up as one of the first Phoenicians who claimed land at what is now 116 West Sherman Street.

The new settlement needed a name if for no other reason than to tell shippers where to send supplies. Some favored Pumpkinsville. Others wanted to call it Mill City after Helling's mill at the asylum site. Salina was still another preference—from the salt marshes along the stream. Swilling's Southern sympathies led him to choose Stonewall.

The erudition of "Lord" Duppa settled the argument. According to the recollections of old Charles T. Hayden, father of the even longer lived politician, a bunch of the boys were gathered convivially one day in 1869 at the Pueblo Grande—the Indian ruin restored in our time by Dwight B. Heard as a museum-monument along the Grand Canal of East Washington Street—when the perennial question was asked, Where *are* we?

Whereupon Duppa clambered to the top of the ruined wall and, raising his cultured voice, proclaimed to somewhat short of a multitude, "As the mythical phoenix rose reborn from its ashes, so shall a great civilization rise here on the ashes of a past civilization. I name thee Phoenix!" [2] It is almost too good to be true, and yet who would dispute the memory of the old miller? Phoenix it was and Phoenix it is.

2. Peplow, *Taming of the Salt*, pp. 17–18.

If one will go there today and stand on the wall where Duppa stood and gaze northeast to Papago Park, he will see in apt conjunction the white-tiled tomb of George Wiley Paul Hunt and the monumental headquarters of the Salt River Project. Far to the southeast at Florence on the Gila, apparent to only the mind's eye, is a rougher tomb, where that other dreamer— Charles Poston—takes his long rest.

Again for reasons unknown Duppa followed Swilling to the Agua Fria, and there on the road to Wickenburg he operated an unofficial stage station. Then and now that region is "an uncompromising piece of desert." Along the same highway stands another modern miracle—Del Webb's Sun City, an "instant city" harboring more than 30,000 fugitives from colder climes.

His lordship's station was a squalid place. Drawing on an early newspaper account, Edward Peplow gave this description:

> The roof was constructed of willows, and the thin, unplastered walls were of ironwood interlaced with rawhide. A few sticks of unpainted furniture were scattered throughout the inside. Guests, when there were any, slept on the dirt floor on blankets taken from a pile stacked in a corner. Guns, ammunition, saddles, whips, and spurs were suspended from the joists and crossbeams. Dogs and mules roamed the establishment. A dwarfish, hairy, and gutteral-voiced cook, whose name is lost in history, prepared the meals for Duppa and guests. They were unusual and surprisingly delicious. When the meals were ready, the hirsute cook would rattle pots, pans, and dutch ovens and bellow out, "Hash pile! Come a'runnin'!" [3]

Duppa's final years were spent, as Poston's were, back in Phoenix, drinking in the back room of Doctor Thibodo's drugstore, and yarning with other old-timers, or loafing under the cottonwoods along the canal. He was described as tall, thin, and very dark, wearing brogans and blue denims, a silver-buckled belt, navy-blue shirt, and black, wide-brimmed hat with flat-topped crown. Except for his speech and lordly manner he would have passed for a typical frontier Arizonan.

He died of pneumonia in 1892. Eighteen years later the Mari-

3. Peplow, *Taming of the Salt*, pp. 19–20.

copa chapter of the Daughters of the American Revolution, overlooking his national origin, reburied him in Greenwood Memorial Park. There on his gravestone are these words:

IN MEMORY OF DARREL DUPPA,
ENGLISH GENTLEMAN AND A PIONEER OF ARIZONA,
WHO NAMED THE CITIES OF PHOENIX AND TEMPE.

Although the city's founder and the city's namer left Phoenix soon thereafter, one to a bad end, the other to a sad end, there were other settlers who stayed and labored to lay the foundations on which Phoenix was to rise and shine. Unlike many of Arizona's earlier pioneers who came to grab and get out, these first Anglo Phoenicians remained in a harmony with their environment which recalled that of the Hohokam. Water and sun and soil and man's toil wrought the resurrection, rather than any dramatic act of God.

Phoenix was situated in a peaceful zone. Its first inhabitants were the docile agricultural tribes—Hohokam, Salado, Pima. We recall that Kearny and Cooke had reported the Pimas at peace with the Anglos in their villages on the Gila. Thus the white farmers came to a land whose only enemies were flood and drought. Canals conquered the former by leading the water back from the vulnerable banks. Drought remained long unmastered.

From 1870 to 1900 the growing number of settlers sought to ameliorate it by building diversion dams across the Salt and the Verde to turn the water onto the thirsty land. In vain. When in flood, those wild rivers were not to be restrained by weirs of rock, planks, and brush. Time and again the weirs were swept away and the Salt roared through to the Gila and on down to the mightiest western river of all—the Colorado.

They were a strong lot, those settlers who resurrected Phoenix. Edward Peplow has gathered accounts of their lives and works in his volume, *The Taming of the Salt.* Too long has the Arizona image been one of cowboy and Indian, bearded prospector, badman, and steely-eyed sheriff. These creative

Phoenicians provide a nobler image. In them were embodied the qualities of fortitude, devotion, and agricultural skill, brought to Arizona by Father Kino.

Some came to farm, others came as laborers or traders, and there were health seekers who thrived in the warm, dry air. There was John Y. T. Smith, whose army service led to contracts for supplying produce to forts Whipple and McDowell, thence to merchandising, and finally to legislating. When asked what his middle initials stood for, he answered genially, "Yours Truly." In 1889 he managed the last move of the capital from Prescott to Phoenix.

There was Columbus Gray, the first to plant citrus and deciduous fruits in the valley in 1868 and who in 1872 sold his uncompleted building to the Goldwaters, thus establishing a commercial dynasty that endures to this day. There was Judge John T. Alsop, who marshaled the orderly growth of Phoenix townsite and who in 1881 became its first mayor. There was William Hancock, a New Englander who came in 1865 as a soldier, stayed to farm, and in 1900 joined in the formation of the Salt River Valley Water Users' Association.

There was Charles Trumbull Hayden, originally a Yankee schoolteacher and Santa Fe trader who freighted in to Tucson in 1858, on to Fort Whipple, and finally built a ferry and mill on the Salt. Hayden's Ferry was renamed Tempe by Darrel Duppa, who likened it fancifully to the Grecian vale of the same name. Today the adobe building (now a restaurant) where the Hayden male heir was born still stands; and although the mill itself is new, the establishment proclaims itself the Hayden Flour Mills.

There was William J. Murphy, who arrived in 1881 as a railroad grading contractor and stayed to extend the canal network with the Arizona Canal and urge the construction of a high dam on the Salt. In 1883 Colonel William Christy's goal was relief from asthma; he then became the first banker and the territorial treasurer who peddled Arizona bonds in the East and joined Governor Brodie in urging President Roosevelt to apply the new Reclamation Act to the valley.

There were surveyor William H. Breckinridge and historian

James H. McClintock, who joined John Norton in finding the site of the Roosevelt Dam. There were also George H. Maxwell, irrigation advocate, and B. A. Fowler, father of the Reclamation Act, and Senator Francis G. Newland of Nevada, champion of the Federal Trade Commission and of federal control of railroads, who spoke for all the arid lands and became known as the Water Boy of the West.

Add Senator Hansbrough of North Dakota, who although he never set foot in Arizona yet joined Newland in sponsoring the bipartisan Reclamation Act. There were Judge Joseph H. Kibbey, father of Arizona's water laws, and John P. Orme, railroad engineer, mule skinner, freighter, and rancher. It was Orme who rode with Roosevelt to the dam's dedication. There they were warned by Bishop Atwood: "You two old sinners won't get any sleep until you say your prayers."

The future of the valley was not assured until the great dam was built, followed by the chain of dams and lakes below and the ensuing security of crops and homes in all seasons and weathers. It is a heroic story of vision, energy, and persistence, in which many strong individuals banded together in common cause. Without the pioneer organizational work of Judge Kibbey on the Salt River Valley Water Users' Association, which became the model for federal reclamation contracts with local farmers, there would have been no development on the scale that led to modern Phoenix and the Salt River Project, which now provides water to thousands of users and hydroelectric power to mining and other ventures.

Today in Arizona it has become politically popular to deplore federal control (though not federal spending when it is in Arizona) in favor of states' rights. From the earliest time of military expenditures to the reclamation budgets and today's massive outlays for defense, Indians, highways, housing, and other social services, Arizona has been aided by revenues from sources other than itself. Uncle Sam is Arizona's most generous relative.[4] At the same time let it be said that reclamation loans

---

4. Federal spending in Arizona in 1974 totaled $3,002,385,000.

to Arizona by the federal government have been scrupulously repaid with interest.

The 1920s ended with Arizona's economy dependent upon copper mining, cattle and sheep raising, lumbering, and upon agriculture in the Salt, Gila, and lower Colorado valleys. Revenue from health seekers and tourists was also a major factor. Manufacturing was nonexistent.

Today the story is different. Manufacturing is the state's leading source of income, followed by mining, agriculture including livestock, and tourism. The Salt River Valley is going the way of Southern California as urbanism supplants agriculture and Phoenix sprawls in all directions. Urban growth turns farmlands into housing tracts and industrial parks, bringing both problems and benefits. Man, the gregarious animal, finds comfort in clustered living, often willing to suffer inconvenience in order to achieve the security of numbers. Where in 1868 Phoenix had thirty residents, in 1976 there are more than a million and still more on the way. Arizona is growing faster than its forty-nine sister states.

There is no need to worry about water for this multitude as long as the irrigated lands continue to be pre-empted by housing and industry. Urbanization and manufacturing use less water than agriculture. Plants such as cotton and alfalfa drink more than people. The need for the billion-dollar Central Arizona Project is predicated on large-scale farming elsewhere in Arizona, as well as on the establishment of new towns.

Phoenix's problems are other than water. Pollution aloft and congestion below are the enemies of healthful, pleasant living. The automobile has come to be the boon and the bane of metropolitan man the world around. He is now the slave of his machine as well as the beneficiary of co-operative living.

Two great social catastrophes, the Depression and World War II, made Arizona what it is today. And in the vast changes thus wrought, in this transformation of Arizona into a predominantly urban-industrial-agribusiness state, ruled from the power base in Phoenix—although many complex social and individual forces were responsible—we perceive one man of destiny who influenced the decades from 1930 as George Wiley Paul Hunt did the first quarter century of statehood.

He was a banker named Bimson—Walter Reed Bimson—and a true Westerner, born in 1891 at Berthoud, Colorado, that foothills town north of Denver where his father was the blacksmith. Walter entered banking as janitor, then clerk in Berthoud's one bank, and began his college education by correspondence, finally completing it at the University of Chicago and the Harvard Business School.

This led to employment with the Harris Trust and Savings Bank of Chicago. There Bimson rose in twelve years to be vice-president; and in charge of commodity credits he made frequent trips to the cotton fields of the Salt River Valley. By the first two decades of this century, cotton had become a major part of the valley's economy.

During his years with Harris Trust, Bimson evolved a progressive philosophy of making banking serve the man in the street, the small customer as well as the corporation. It was a philosophy he was unable to practice at the conservative Chicago bank, and it led to his acceptance of the presidency of a small Phoenix bank. "This is my country," he wrote to his father with certainty akin to that felt by Brigham Young when he first came to Utah.[5]

When on the last day of December in 1932 Walter Bimson arrived in Arizona to head the Valley National Bank, he could not have chosen a more dramatic and desperate time to put into practice his philosophy that had been rejected by the Harris bank. First, however, he had to face an immediate crisis. When in the night he heard by radio that Governor Rolph would close all of California's banks on the morrow, Bimson knew that swift action in Arizona was imperative. At that time—and only somewhat less today—Arizona was economically tied to Cali-

5. Don Dedera, "Arizona's Indispensable Man," *Arizona Highways* 49:22–29 (April 1973).

fornia, especially in mutual banking ventures. If Arizona's banks too were not closed, their assets would be siphoned off to California. And so Banker Bimson prevailed upon Governor Moeur immediately to close all banks throughout Arizona, thus forestalling a run on them by depositors small and large, in and out of state.

This was no small feat for a young newcomer. It involved waking the governor before dawn and convincing him to let him (Bimson) draw the proclamation of closing. Not every bank in Arizona obeyed the governor's order. Down in Cochise County, stronghold of the copper clan, old Dr. Douglas's son, James S., known as Rawhide Jimmy, refused to close his banks in Bisbee and Douglas. "Nothing wrong with my banks," he growled. "Damned if I'll close them." The governor's proclamation was illegal, he maintained; only a legislative act could compel him to comply. The governor threatened to call out the National Guard. Before a confrontation could occur, the moratorium was ended.[6]

In this first act by Walter Bimson is seen the vision, vigor, and decisiveness of a born leader, and it foretold the bold acts of good judgment with which he directed the Valley Bank for many years.

There at the bottom of the Depression, Bimson put his philosophy to work. Its basic credo was "Lend money!" He knew that the circulation of hoarded money, the lifeblood of the economy, was the best medicine for the ailing state. He moved his desk to the front door of the home office, and from there by many liberal innovations he made banking serve the common man. "Master of the calculated risk," he called himself. Frozen funds were made to flow. Branches were opened throughout the state.

Arizona's industrial growth was caused by World War II. It was a dynamic growth in which the Valley National Bank was a

6. William H. Hervey, Jr., "When the Banks Closed: Arizona's Bank Holiday of 1933," *Arizona and the West* 10:2 (Summer 1968).

financial keystone in the development that made Phoenix a center in the manufacture of aircraft and electronic components. It began with the military's discovering the flatlands west, north, and east of Phoenix to be ideal for training purposes. This in turn led companies such as Sperry Rand and Airesearch to locate plants there during and after the war. In addition, thousands of servicemen lured by sunshine and relaxed living returned to Arizona after the war, thus providing the new industries with labor and the stores with customers.

Bimson also persuaded the state to change its tax laws to favor industry. He kept lending money especially to agriculture, and always with calculated risk. To him an honest face was good collateral. No account was too small to be scorned, no potential locator in the Salt River Valley was given other than a red-carpet welcome. Two that became Arizona's largest builders and manufacturers, Del Webb and Motorola, were staked by the Bimson bank.

This postwar proliferation of valley industry led to the expansion of Arizona State College (which grew from the original Tempe Normal School) into Arizona State University. In 1956 the regents were waited on by a committee composed of Walter Bimson, Daniel Noble of Motorola, and K. S. Brown of the AFL-CIO. They pointed out that the growing electronics industry needed mathematicians, chemists, physicists, and electrical engineers; and that the Tempe campus was the logical place to train them. A new engineering school thus came into being. General Electric next sponsored a computer center on campus. Solar energy was another field of experimentation that belonged naturally in the Valley of the Sun. From the first, A.S.U. was a leader in the education of teachers, and latterly of lawyers.

Tempe's coming of age as a second major campus was delayed by the mother institution in Tucson in the same way that Berkeley slowed the growth of UCLA. Yet it is also true that A.S.U. benefited from the precedents established by the University of Arizona. If Arizona maintains its prodigious growth, it will need at least two state universities of high scholarly standards. This could be the destiny of the Tempe campus. Its fulfillment depends upon several factors: the will of the people, the state's finances, the wisdom of the regents, and finally, leadership of the kind that brought the University of Arizona to a high level and is keeping it there.

A third four-year school, Northern Arizona University, is at Flagstaff, amidst the tall pines. Forestry and the fine arts lend distinction to this smaller campus. Arizona has also developed a two-year community-college system throughout the state.

There was another crucial factor that ensured Phoenix's growth as well as the growth of all Arizona. Some argue that it was the single most important event in Arizona's phenomenal growth. This was the postwar perfection of refrigerated air conditioning that changed the way of life for dwellers on the desert, and especially for those in the Valley of the Sun, where the heat of summer sent all who could to seek relief at seashore and mountain. Now the city became a year-round abode. This was of supreme importance to industry, as it made possible sustained production schedules.[7]

Because of its location Phoenix was a logical distribution center for the Southwest from Los Angeles and San Francisco to Denver, Albuquerque, and El Paso. California manufacturers also found inventory tax-exempt warehousing in Phoenix to be cheaper as well as more strategically located. The city was no longer the hapless colony of California's two metropolii.

The most important factor in this growth was air conditioning. The most important individual was Walter Bimson. He was a refreshing change from the stereotype of tight-fisted, stiff-collared, hard-to-see banker. He was more than a banker. As a member of the statewide universities' board of regents, instigator of civic and cultural enterprises, patron and collector of

7. The best account of air conditioning in Arizona is Bert M. Fireman's succinct "Urbanization and Home Comfort," William R. Noyes, editor, *Progress in Arizona,* unpaged.

Western art, outdoorsman and crack shot, Bimson was indeed a man to match Arizona's mountains.

He is not the only heroic figure to emerge in the Salt River Valley. There is also Barry Goldwater, a third-generation Arizonan descended from pioneer merchants who came in the 1860s. We must go back to George Wiley Paul Hunt to find another Arizonan who dominated the state's political life for as long. Not only the state's spokesman, Barry Goldwater became a national voice for conservatism.

It was he who led the revolution that ended the Democrats' single-party hold on Arizona politics. This was not the conventional conservative-radical shift. The Democrats in Arizona were long akin to Southern conservatives. As ardently as he championed Labor and courted the working man, Governor Hunt's continuing power came from a pragmatic alliance with the dominant economic interests which gave him the gubernatorial chair and them the legislative seats.

Beginning in the 1940s Goldwater rose through Phoenix civic offices to Republican party leadership. In 1950 he managed the campaign of Howard Pyle, a genial radio figure, and saw him become the first Republican governor in twenty-two years. Goldwater then rode the Eisenhower wave to defeat Ernest McFarland for a seat in the United States Senate. This led to his unsuccessful candidacy for the presidency in 1964.

Barry Goldwater is an independent politician, speaking his own mind, often shooting from the lip, and unbeholden to rightwing radicals who would make him their spokesman. Sometimes too outspoken for his own political good, as in the presidential campaign when he attacked Social Security and the TVA at the same time that he supported the Central Arizona Project, Goldwater has always opposed big government. Motivated first by patriotism and party loyalty, his role in the Watergate scandal was painfully ambivalent, as he was eventually compelled to "blow the whistle" on President Nixon.

Goldwater's devotion to his state and its native races was never ambivalent. For his love of the history, lore, and geography of the Grand Canyon state, he became widely known as Mr. Arizona. Integrity and courage are his hallmarks.

His political support was twofold, from voters and from the Phoenix press of Eugene Pulliam, a conservative Indianapolis journalist who came to Arizona, acquired the *Republic* and the *Gazette* in 1946 and made them his instruments in a drive to create a viable two-party system. His electoral support came from the postwar migration of a new middle class of professional, managerial, and skilled workers attracted to the Salt River Valley by the Bimson boom. Drawn largely from the Republican Midwest and conservative by nature, this new generation of Arizonans provided the votes that in 1966 put the Republicans in control of the Arizona senate, house and governorship, though in 1974 Raul Castro, a Mexican-born American from Tucson, defeated the Republican candidate from Phoenix, and the Democrats regained the governor's chair.

Let us suppose that Goldwater's ambition had not led him onto the national stage where, although he became a powerful figure, he was never able to command an effective majority. If he had been content to remain at the gubernatorial level, he might have held the capitol even longer than did George the Seventh.

Mine is not the prejudice of many Arizonans, especially in Tucson, who regard Phoenix with suspicion and scorn. Thus San Francisco looks down on Los Angeles.

Meanwhile Phoenix goes its lusty way, swallowing fields and farms and fulfilling its destiny in the manner of all great cities from London to Los Angeles. The benefits to the entire state of such power centers are often ignored while their negative effects are being deplored. Revenues from Phoenix's prosperity flow statewide. Without them the standard of living and the educational benefits enjoyed throughout Arizona would be of a lower order. All growth and progress are at a price.

The disadvantages of urbanism are obvious—noxious air, crowded streets, loss of privacy, slums—and those of Phoenix are there to see. We can only trust that man's ingenuity proves able to overcome these detriments to the good life in a big city.

The virtues of largeness are often obscured by the vices. A big city is vital, and progress comes from vitality, from strength. A strong organism is a growing organism. A great city is a magnet and also a dynamo, discharging energy in all directions. Phoenix is indeed akin to Los Angeles. In another generation or two, and with good fortune, there could be a cultural flowering in the Valley of the Sun similar to that which is happening today in Los Angeles.

Great size creates wealth, and this in turn affords leisure and reflection and an environment in which the arts flourish. Painting, sculpture, music, drama, and architecture will come increasingly to further the civilizing of Greater Phoenix. As time passes, there will be a better "mix" of the generations, more young people and permanent residents whose roots go deep in the valley. Layers of cultural humus will accumulate, in which creativity finds nourishment.

Literature's day has yet to come, the day when Phoenix produces a writer such as Raymond Chandler, who employed the detective story to immortalize the landscape and mores of Los Angeles in the 1920s and 1930s. If literature is writing of unusual power, truth, and beauty, there is yet no literature about Phoenix. Its writer, when he or she comes, need not be a native nor even a longtime resident, yet must he have a root system to penetrate blacktop and spread like the mesquite's. Such a writer must also have strong feelings about the environment, of either love or hate or, ambivalently, both, and a mastery of language to transmit these feelings to the reader.

Such a spokesman sees and says in prose of power and grace. Secure at the heart of the whirlwind he measures the city's ebb and flow, recounts its grandeur and misery, and recreates his vision as Dickens did of London, Balzac of Paris, Joyce of Dublin, and Chandler of Los Angeles. He or she is apt to be an unlikely person, postman or professor, yet empowered with perception, absorptive capacity, and stamina, a writer given to working secretly in the night when the rest of the world sleeps.

No crystal ball can reveal when such a writer will appear or who he or she will be. The inevitable voice could come sooner or later, now or never. We can only wait and wonder when, if ever, that one will come to give voice and soul to the city which is at once consuming and recreating the Valley of the Sun.

Meanwhile there is beauty there in the spreading city—the green of growing things along wide streets and winding canals, of palm, oleander, citrus, and olive; the desert-colored architecture inspired by Frank Lloyd Wright in the Arizona Biltmore with its glowing murals by Maynard Dixon, and in Tempe that same architect's wedding cake, the Grady Gammage auditorium; while downtown the high buildings, those proud *casas grandes,* shine in the sun. Imaginative fountains and daring sculpture adorn the new Civic Plaza. The city is also blessed with the Heard Museum, which serenely displays the art and artifacts of the earliest Arizonans.

There is life and beauty in Phoenix, and if the flow of water and the flow of money continue, it might someday prove a Southwestern renaissance city. When, O Lord, how soon?

> Will Time say nothing but I told you so?
> If I could tell you I would let you know.[8]

8. W. H. Auden, "If I Could Tell You." Copyright 1945 by W. H. Auden. Reprinted from *Collected Shorter Poems* 1927–1957, by W. H. Auden, by permission of Random House, Inc.

8

The Old Pueblo

$\mathcal{T}$HE melting pot that wouldn't,'' is how Bernard Fontana describes Arizona.[1] Although they meet in superficial contact, its three peoples—Indian, Hispano, Anglo—do not fuse. While there is some intermarrying among the latter two, it is not a common practice. Nowhere is this essential separateness truer than in Tucson, a town that has suffered repeated cultural shock as its possessors have passed in a long procession. Hohokam, Pima, Apache, Papago, Spaniard, Mexican, Confederate—all have had their day in the desert sun. And now in our time there is strife among the Anglos for the power that will pass from them too. Democrats, Republicans, conservationists, developers, men and women struggle among themselves.

Loss of the capital twice to Prescott and finally to Phoenix has never really been accepted by Tucson, admittedly the oldest and surely the proudest modern settlement in Arizona, excluding the older Hopi villages. The Old Pueblo is its fond sobriquet. Tucson has always regarded itself as the cultural capital—Pop McKale, the humorous University of Arizona coach, used to speak of it as the Athens of Arizona—and boasted of its

---

1. Bernard L. Fontana, "The Melting Pot That Wouldn't: Ethnic Groups in the American Southwest Since 1846," *American Indian Culture and Research Journal* 1:2 (1974).

Hispanic antecedents, although its original lineage is Indian, its true "first families" the Papagos. Tucson's aboriginal origin is there in the hill that gave the place its name.

This black volcanic formation across the Santa Cruz is now called "A" Mountain from the university's letter which disfigures its side. At its base among the mesquites on either side of the river was an ancient *ranchería*—a scattering of huts occupied by a mixture of Pimas, Papagos, and Sopaipuris—called Chukson.

In Papago, *chuk* means "black," *son* means "hill." Confusion arises from the fact that *son* can also mean "spring." Hence Chukson is said also to signify "black spring." The best evidence for "black hill" comes from there now being on the Papago Reservation a village called Ali Chukson—Little Tucson. There is no spring there; there *is* a black hill.

In the time of the Spaniards and until recently, the Papagos had no written language, and so the missionaries had various ways of spelling and pronouncing Chukson. Tucson came at last to be preferred by them and the Anglos. Today the Hispanos' pronunciation of Tukesone is closest to the original. Anglos call it Toóson or Toosón, and it is often misspelled Tuscon.

As a Spanish pueblo, Tucson is the same age as the American republic. After Anza's departure from Tubac in September 1775 en route to Alta California, the order was issued to transfer the garrison to Tucson better to protect the mission at San Xavier from the Apaches; and so early in 1776 the little company of soldiers marched downriver and formed the Royal Presidio of San Agustín de Tucson. The few puebloans who dwelled within the watch-towered walls that were built in the next several years were afforded only fragile sanctuary from the marauders. Soldiers assigned to the presidio often complained that they spent more time making adobes than they did in military pursuits.

Today nothing remains of that original mud pueblo, although the archaeologists have discovered where the walls ran and beneath them have unearthed the charred remains of an Indian pithouse and fire hearth. By tree-ring dating and Carbon 14 tests the antiquity of Chukson as a site of Indian habitation has been extended back as far as A.D. 700.

If we would see an adobe pueblo such as Tucson was two centuries ago, we must travel to Mexico or Spain, although TV antennae now form a different skyline even there. Nearer by may be seen Papago *rancherías* little different from prehistoric Chukson. They are changing as modern building materials replace mesquite limbs, saguaro ribs, and canes of the ocotillo.

Along the Santa Cruz where it runs through the city, the mesquite thicket, erstwhile haunt of the white-winged dove, was long since cut for firewood. Today the riverbanks are a dumpland, although the city hopes to transform this squalor into an urban park as San Antonio did with its river. Until now Tucson has turned its back on the river and closed its eyes to the humbler people who inhabit the western bank, while it continues to sprawl eastward in housing projects, or conceals its growth on the arboreal slopes—the Spanish *bajada*—of the Santa Catalinas.

A massive ingestion of federal money has "renewed" the moribund urban center with imposing government and office buildings and auditoria, a hotel, restaurant, and bazaar. This was done by demolishing much of what remained of the Barrio Libre, the old Mexican town center—the "free neighborhood where anything goes." A study of the Old Pueblo made by the university's architecture students concluded, "The barrio today does not contain a multitude of significant places of major historical importance. Its importance is in the collective whole or spirit that the barrio expresses in its demonstration of the traditional elements and modes of Mexican-American life." [2]

The uncared-for, sun-dried adobes of which the barrio was built wear away in the wind and the rain. When in preparation for the bicentennial it was planned to restore a territorial gover-

2. *Barrio Historico, Tucson* (Tucson: University of Arizona School of Architecture, 1972), p. 10.

nor's home in Tucson, only the Frémont adobe had survived, and it was a ruin. The truth is that Frémont never inhabited it; he rented it for his daughter to live in as he departed from Arizona in 1881 never to return. She too left soon thereafter. When the restoration culminated in a ceremony to dedicate the *casa de gobernador,* the honored guests were the numerous descendants of the Sosa family, which had inhabited the adobe in territorial times.

Life goes on in the vestigial barrio south of the Community Center. There some of the old modes persist in those few blocks now preserved as an historic zone, although some owners would have preferred to sell their land for high-rise apartments. Others saw a refurbished barrio as a lucrative tourist attraction. Because of overcrowding, many of the younger Hispano families have moved across the river, leaving the old folks behind.

Roundabout the city stand those presences that lend majesty and character to Tucson's setting—the mountains that have stood for a million years. Their names make a beautiful litany: Santa Catalinas, Tanque Verdes, Rincons, Whetstones, Huachucas, Santa Ritas, Sierritas, Baboquívaris, Tucsons, Tortolitas, and Silverbells. The highest of them rise through zones of piñon and juniper to oak and pine and winter snow.

Not only do they exalt the landscape, their rainy runoff creates the table of groundwater upon which Tucson's life has been based. Unlike Phoenix, which depends upon the flow of its river system, Tucson's water is pumped from wells that keep falling as mining, agriculture, and town consume increasing amounts and the subterranean flow of the Santa Cruz diminishes.

Tucson's economy is neither agricultural nor industrial like its northern neighbor's, and its desert is arboreal. As the land rises toward Mexico, elevating Tucson 1300 feet higher than Phoenix, more rainfall means greener land. Dust blows where man has broken the earth's fabric. These environmental differences separate the two cities, close though they be on the map and in the unifying ways of urban life.

Yet man cannot live on mountains and well water alone. What has made Tucson Arizona's second city? Not agriculture. The cotton fields lie farther north into Pinal County. Pecan orchards and stock ranches line the shores of the river toward the Mexican border, while copper mines unearth the hills to the west.

In the days of the territory the town was a trading center for mines, ranches, and military posts. As the termination of Mexico's northern thrust, it was crossed by the westering Anglos who created there a cultural eddy of enduring vitality. Tucson's early families were mercantilers. There was Estevan Ochoa, originally a Santa Fe trader, and Solomon Warner who opened the first store in 1856. Ochoa became a strong link between the Hispanos and Anglos and helped Governor Safford found the first public schools. Ochoa's partner was Pinckney Randolph Tully, who later became a banker, territorial treasurer, and mayor of Tucson, and a founder of the *Weekly Star*.

Those pioneer eastern European traders, who began as suppliers of "everything from carbine needles to pulpits" and who settled in Tucson and elsewhere in Arizona, included the Goldwaters, Zeckendorfs, Ivancovichs, Mansfelds, Solomons, Drachmans, Jacobses, and Steinfelds. They were the merchant princes of the frontier who came and worked and stayed. Their profits were invested in the region and helped it become civilized. Today some of their descendants continue the process. Ronstadt is still another esteemed family in Tucson's pioneer annals.

Likewise the scions of early immigrants from Mexico today form an important element of Tucson's culture. The Ochoas, Carrillos, Aguirres, Eliases, Jácomes, Sosas, Pachecos, and Laoses are among the city's Hispano "first families." And there is María Urquides, a third-generation Arizonan whose forebears came in the eighteenth century from Spanish Basque Pamplona by way of Alamos, Sonora. A graduate of the University of Arizona and old Tempe State College, with further study in Mexico and California, this strong woman has given her life to teaching and administration in the Tucson public schools. She proudly acknowledges the mingled blood of Spain, Mexico, and the Pimería Alta. At the same time she recognizes that the United States provided the kind of intellectual opportunity for women that she sought.

Throughout the years there has been some intermarrying among Hispanos and Anglos. Two of Governor Safford's three wives were Hispanos. Governor Raul Castro has an Anglo wife.

In Tucson one is always aware that Mexico is near. Called Ambos Nogales, the twin border cities of Nogales, Arizona, and Nogales, Sonora, witness a constant flow of people back and forth between the two countries. The tempo of Tucson and the city's essential character are inevitably affected by this nearness to Mexico. Not much more than a century ago there was no border; the land was all Mexico; and before that it was the land of the Upper Pimas, the Pimería Alta of Padre Kino.

Phoenix is a very different city. It has no Indo-Hispano "aristocracy" comparable to Tucson's. Most of the Mexicans who came to the Salt River Valley during the past hundred years were laborers, and this pattern of immigration continues.

In the early years, despite its expansive setting of river and mountains, Tucson was a poor place, hardly more than a village with crude hotels, saloons, stables, and general stores. In 1857 the first dam was built on the Santa Cruz to power Solomon Warner's grinding mill and create Silver Lake, which became a social center for boating, bathing, and picnicking. Sweet water from the springs called El Ojito was peddled through the dusty streets of the pueblo.

By 1870 there were only 3200 inhabitants, mostly Hispanos. In her diary Mrs. Granville Oury, wife of the Confederate general, expressed the feelings of cultured immigrants when she wrote, "Tucson is certainly the most forlorn, dreary, desolate, God-forsaken spot of earth ever trodden by the foot of man." [3]

It was also a rough and lawless place, its saloons spewing

3. Mrs. Granville Oury, "Diary," *Arizona Historical Review* 6:1 (1935) 61.

brawlers into the mud or dust at all hours of day and night, rivaled only by Los Angeles as the Southwest's most iniquitous sink.

The Pepys of the pueblo—albeit an ignorant and drunken one in contrast to the brilliant and amoral Sam—was the soldier-butcher-saloonist-janitor, George O. Hand, who came with the army in the 1860s and stayed until his death in 1887. Although a diarist without the least literary distinction, he had an eye for the trivia and troubles of life on the frontier and for the doings, especially scandalous, of his fellow Tucsonans drunk and sober.

Here is one of his vignettes of Tucson ninety years ago: "Warm and cloudy. Went to breakfast at 7 o'clock. Found Juana and all the children crying. Foster accidentally struck his head against the bird cage, knocked the bottom out; the bird went on the floor and the cat caught it, and it was dead in an instant. The cat died also very soon after. Rum at noon. 2 p.m. still at it. 2.30 adjourned till tomorrow. I read all the afternoon. Dinner at 4.40. Stayed home this evening and read till late."

A few more entries of 1886 reveal Hand's flair for the sardonic:

Sunday, August 22. Hot and getting hotter. Tried to sleep, but failed.
Wednesday, August 25. Fine morning. No water. Hell to pay in the courthouse.
Friday, August 27. Nothing worth recording.
Sunday, August 29. Fine day, but a little tight. Took a walk to the park. Came home early.
Sunday, Otober 3. Churches are full tonight and saloons are doing poor biz.[4]

When in the 1960s the *Arizona Daily Star* printed Hand's entries of a hundred years earlier, it was deemed necessary to bowdlerize them. Too many leading Tucsonans (whose descendants still lead) were observed as regular patrons of the local brothels. Of somewhat more historical value are Hand's entries

4. Collection of extracts from *Arizona Daily Star* of various dates in University of Arizona Library, Dept. of Special Collections.

as janitor in the Pima county courthouse, where he was privy to the town's social transgressions.

Few traditions have survived from the early days. The Wishing Shrine is one, although its antiquity has been questioned. There are various versions of its origin. One is that when in the 1870s an Hispano husband found his wife with their boarder, he chased the younger man through the streets and killed him with an axe. The version which Arnulfo Trejo believes to be the most authentic is that the victim was really innocent and had been comforting the woman who had fled to his room during a violent thunderstorm. A mesquite crucifix had been shaken from the wall and at the moment the husband burst in, the boarder had been piously replacing it. He took to his heels still holding the cross, slipped in the muddy street and fell on the thorns and was pierced through the heart.

The site of his alleged death became an unsanctified shrine called El Tiradito (The Outcast). A century later the shrine is still believed to possess the power of granting wishes to those whose candles burn through the night. Thanks to Professor Trejo and his committee, El Tiradito is now protected as an Historical Landmark.

Bishop Salpointe's Cathedral of San Agustín fell on evil times. After the turn of the century it became in the words of an early Tucsonan, "a hotel, a cheap hotel, cheaper hotel, whorehouse, taxi stand, garage, service station, bootleg headquarters, fight arena, etc." When in 1936 it was condemned as a public menace and was being torn down, Tucsonan George W. Chambers, with an eye to historical preservation, bought the stones and rose-window frame of the arched portal for $75 and built them into his home. In 1973 he gave them to the Arizona Historical Society for the main entrance to its enlarged headquarters. Although neither truly antique nor beautiful, the portal is nevertheless a symbol of Tucson's belated efforts to preserve its past.[5]

5. George W. Chambers and C. L. Sonnichsen, *San Agustín, First Cathedral Church in Arizona* (Tucson: Arizona Historical Society, 1974), pp. 48–49.

In spite of sporadic violence, scandal, and squalor in the Old Pueblo's early years, decency generally prevailed. There were those men of industry and women of virtue whose faithful toil built an enduring community. The coming of the railroad on March 12, 1880, ended the town's isolation and hastened the trend toward civilization. It also provided the occasion for a cork-popping banquet at which Poston was the toastmaster. Folklore has it that he helped Mayor Leatherwood draft a cablegram to the Pope, duly sanctioned by Bishop Salpointe, in which a blessing was asked on the Ancient and Honorable Pueblo of Tucson. This inspired a bit of rough humor when a reply purportedly sent from Rome by the Papal Secretary was read aloud at the banquet. The blessing was conferred but then the question was asked, "Where in hell is Tucson?" [6]

A century later that's still a good question as the city spins off in all directions, mostly eastward toward the Rincons. Booming new shopping centers such as El Con—built on the site of the old hotel El Conquistador—now provide the beat that once came from the heart of the old town. More than concrete buildings and tourist attractions are needed to re-center the city. Freeway and railway split Tucson in two. Communication between the parts is uncertain as many streets end at the tracks.

Northeast of these dividers is Anglo, southwest is Hispano. There is little meaningful meeting of the twain. The lifestyle of the Catalina foothills and of the eastern flatlands resembles that of Phoenix and Los Angeles, in which the dominant activities are poolside, linkside, and at bridge and buffet table, while the west side of the Santa Cruz south from St. Mary's Road is largely Sonoran in language, habits, and, unfortunately, in slowness of economic growth.

There is a book that enshrines the soul of this humble side of the river. It was written by Richard Summers who was born

6. Bernice Cosulich, *Tucson* (Tucson: Arizona Silhouettes, 1960), pp. 243–244. In the absence of a history of the city, this collection of essays is the best source on the early years.

under a star that never danced for him. He was a professor at odds with the university establishment. He was a writer who taught writing yet whose million words proved chaff on the wind. The few kernels that remained are his novel called *Dark Madonna,* a story of the wrong side of the river and its ordeal in the Depression. With Eastern publishing and promotion it might have proved another *Tortilla Flat* which it resembles, although it lacks the bawdy humor of the Steinbeck tale. Obscure publication in Idaho as well as its rejection by the right side of the river, doomed the book to failure.

A university student, Patrick Murphy, wrote the best appreciation of *Dark Madonna.* Here is the conclusion of it:

> A freeway now bifurcates the neighborhood of which Richard Summers wrote, a mocking river of concrete and gasoline fumes that separates the old town from the gap-toothed Tucson Mountains as the now-dry Santa Cruz never did. All through the night the lighted temples to government and recreation stand on the ground where Lupe passed barefoot and dazed on her return from the *bruja's* hovel. Avoiding these lights, figures still pass dazed and lost with drugs and alcohol, the children and grandchildren of Lupe and Maria and Yoga and Mucio, the glare of the great buildings a reminder of their light-year's separation from the world Richard Summers wrote of. Tucson has changed greatly in the forty years since *Dark Madonna.* What the reviewers found 'sociological' in the novel is now historical. The poorer though we may be for the passing of the culture portrayed *in extremis* in *Dark Madonna,* we are the richer for having this record of it. It is a greater contribution to the wealth of Tuscon than all the great buildings and all their lights.[7]

Amtrak now provides passenger service over the Southern Pacific tracks as a train comes through three times a week on the Los Angeles-to-New Orleans run. This is the Sunset Limited, the former crack train on which Colonel Hooker and his fellow kings of cattle, copper, and cotton once rode in grand style. Freight is now the railroad's profitable business, and the long trains pass through the city by day and by night.

7. Patrick Murphy, "Richard Summers' *Dark Madonna:* An Appreciation." unpublished essay, quoted with permission of the author.

Interstate Highway 10 is also a thoroughfare for the movement of everything—tourists, migrants, machinery, chemicals, furniture, livestock, fruits, and vegetables. Like Phoenix, Tucson is crippled by auto traffic, although without the auto Tucson would be a forlorn desert town. On windless mornings the usual sixty-mile visibility is sometimes reduced by pollution.

The Old Pueblo depends upon a few main sources for its economic health. The first is the university—once the sop thrown to Tucson when the more lucrative insane asylum went to Phoenix and the normal school to Tempe. Now grown to nearly 30,000 students and a corresponding faculty and staff, the University of Arizona provides the city's richest single source of income. The air-force base of Davis-Monthan, nearby Fort Huachuca, and the related Hughes missile plant, are the other large payrolls. Affluent winter residents and seasonal tourists spend millions of dollars in the city. Miners who live in and near Tucson are also a considerable source of revenue.

The university and the climate give Tucson more character and prosperity than its historical and ethnic antiquity. Without the university's cohesive power, the town would be merely another prosperous desert resort—a Scottsdale or a Palm Springs. University and climate are eminently compatible. Students and faculty who are drawn to southern Arizona by its salubrious weather often remain to enrich the community.

Tucson's sometimes affected pride in its Indian and Hispanic past, and its concern for the present welfare of these races, owes more to the university than to the fiestas and rodeos that are periodically celebrated. The university's research has been directed toward the environment in which it finds itself, to the fields of agriculture, hydrology, mining, astronomy, optics, atmospheric physics, anthropology and archaeology—all subjects pertinent to the state and particularly to the Sonoran Desert.

The University of Arizona began as a humble mining and agricultural school sited on a small tract of raw creosote desert near town, donated by two gamblers and a saloon keeper. Although authorized in 1885, it did not begin instruction, including high school classes, until 1891. The prime mover in locating the university in Tucson and its first regent was J. G. Mansfeld, the pioneer merchant who opened his stationery and cigar store in 1869. The first building was the structure which, as Old Main, still stands at the hub of the campus. There are those who regard this classic territorial, whose architect was C. H. Creighton of Phoenix, as the handsomest building in town, although the old El Paso and Southwestern depot is also a favorite of some.

The new school attracted able professors such as Robert H. Forbes in agricultural chemistry, William P. Blake in mining geology, G. E. P. Smith in hydrology (who, like Forbes, lived past 100), Byron Cummings in archaeology, and Frank C. Lockwood in English. Its first professional librarian, Estelle Lutrell, was a bibliographical scholar who created a fine Arizona collection, listed the territorial newspapers, and wrote a monograph on San Xavier del Bac.

The science of tree-ring dating, known as dendochronology, was pioneered by astronomer A. E. Douglass. Long-staple Pima cotton was first propagated by the university and the United States Department of Agriculture. Dean Cummings, and later Emil Haury and his colleagues, made Tucson a distinguished center for research in the archaeo-anthropology of the Southwest—perhaps the highest rated of the university's departments.

Since World War II the university has explored new frontiers on earth and in the sky. Because of the clear atmosphere and proximity of the university, the National Science Foundation, with the strong support of Senator Carl Hayden, established a national observatory on Kitt Peak at the northern end of the Baboquívari range. Operated by a consortium of universities called AURA, including Arizona, California, Caltech, Chicago, Harvard, Illinois, Indiana, Michigan, Ohio State, Princeton, Texas, Wisconsin, and Yale, this center for astronomical research has proliferated in a score of installations on the nearly 7000-foot mountain. Because of the observatory's location on the reservation, a "treaty" was made with the Papago tribe whereby the Indians retained firewood rights on the mountain and profits from the museum shop. They also received an initial payment of $25,000 and an annual rental of $2550, half of which goes to the Schuk Toak school district in which the observatory is located.

In conjunction with the Steward Observatory on campus and the Lunar and Planetary Laboratory of the university and their component observatories on the nearby mountains, the Kitt Peak National Observatory has become a leader in the probes of outer space.

Kitt Peak is now a mecca for the world's astronomers. Tucson has shown its appreciation of the observatory's importance by adopting legislation which requires all outdoor illumination to be shielded from above.

Distinction has also been gained by the university in Arid Lands studies, interdisciplinary in nature and international in scope. They reach out to kindred agencies in Africa, Asia, and Australia. Hopes for peace are furthered by such studies, as they bring visiting Arab and Israeli scholars together in efforts relating to their desert ecology.

Controlled-environment agriculture, directed by Carl Hodges, is being carried out in such widely separated places as the Quechan Indian Reservation on the Colorado River (tomatoes) and the sheikdom of Abu Dhabi on the Red Sea (vegetable crops). A similar shrimp culture has been started in Mexico at Puerto Peñasco on the Gulf of California and in the environs of Tucson. Weather modification, water resources and watershed management, crop control, and ways of repairing the destruction of range and forest, are other areas in which the university's leadership extends beyond the borders of Arizona.

As its achievements and recognition have increased, so has the university attracted scholars from around the world, including the Dutch astronomers Bart Bok and the late Gerard Kuiper. In this age of rapid transportation and instant communication, it is not anachronistic to find an Antarctic authority based on the Sonoran Desert. After all, Antarctica is a polar desert. Such is

Laurence M. Gould, the grizzled geologist who "retired" to the University of Arizona fifteen years ago.

If Tucson could choose today between having the capital or the university, the latter would undoubtedly be the city's overwhelming choice.

If Tucson never had a Bimson, neither has Phoenix had a Mathews. From 1924 to 1969 William R. Mathews was the publisher of the Democratic *Arizona Daily Star*. He made it into more than a local journal. Under Mathews the *Star* attained, although on a lesser scale, a position of respect and influence in Arizona akin to that once held by the *San Francisco Chronicle*. Such power is never permanent. Today in Arizona and in California, the comparable journals are the *Arizona Republic*, one of the two Pulliam papers, and the *Los Angeles Times*.

Chance brought Mathews to Arizona. His birth and schooling were Midwestern. As a Marine captain in World War I, he received the Croix de Guerre for bravery under fire. After the war he became a managerial newspaperman in San Francisco and Santa Barbara. When he heard that a similar job was open in Tucson, he was in no hurry to inquire about it. When after a year had passed he found it still open, he decided to move to Tucson; and in 1924 he and Ralph Ellinwood borrowed money and bought the ailing *Arizona Daily Star*—bought it from Phelps Dodge which, seeking a better public image, was disposing of some of its properties. With Ellinwood as editor and Mathews as manager they set out to prove that they weren't "copper-collared." They succeeded. When in 1930 Ellinwood died, his partner became editor and owner, and the *Star* of Mathews began its rise.

It rose high. In addition to nonpartisan news coverage, the *Star* became conscience voice and call to action of the state's majority party. Mathews usually wrote the lead editorials. They were clear and emphatic as would be expected from a former Marine officer. His endorsement was sought and when gained was often decisive. His interests were local, statewide, regional, national, and foreign, and in that order.

Bill Mathews was cultured, shrewd, partisan, proud, and tough. His fuse was short, his boiling point low. Hal Marshall, the former assistant city editor of the *Star* and now head of the university's news bureau, tells of coming back to the paper one night, and seeing the publisher's inviolable parking space empty and believing the boss had gone home, he wheeled into the empty stall and went on up to his desk. Soon a reporter rushed in to say that Mr. Mathews was downstairs letting the air out of the assistant city editor's tires. Whereupon Marshall hurried down and was greeted with, "Glad you came. I was getting tired."

As a member of the Board of Regents Mathews worked for more than the Tucson campus. When the colleges in Flagstaff and Tempe were given university status, he strove for a balance between the competitive institutions. His finest achievement was in seeing the state's first medical school established in Tucson. As the power of the Salt River Valley was brought to bear on locating the school in Phoenix, a fight ensued. A deciding factor was the Commonwealth Fund committee's conclusion that the scholarly standards of the University of Arizona made Tucson the inevitable location, although it was recognized that the population of the Phoenix area offered a greater source of clinical material.

Another decisive factor was the weight of the Phoenix press, which Pulliam finally threw on the Tucson scales. One view is that this was the result of a Mathews-Pulliam deal in which the former agreed to support the Central Arizona Project in return for the latter's conceding the medical school to Tucson. A source close to Pulliam told me that this was the case. A source close to Mathews told me that it was not. When the two publishers' archives are finally made public, the truth will perhaps be revealed.

Mathews led a campaign to raise private funds that would ensure the balance from federal sources. He was successful beyond all hopes but his own. Individuals, organizations, and businesses throughout Arizona, blandished and bludgeoned by the publisher, gave more than $3,000,000—a large sum for a small state, but in the end a mere fraction of the $32,000,000 it cost to build the enormous facility.

Today the Arizona Medical Center looms near campus. With its teaching and research units and university hospital, it forms the largest public building in Arizona. It is also a monument to Dr. Merlin K. DuVal, seasoned medical administrator brought by President Harvill to plan and staff the new facility.

Mathews died in 1969 at the age of 76. His likeness may be seen in bronze at the entrance of the Center's Basic Sciences building. The inscription reads: "The University and the Community present this plaque to William R. Mathews who dedicated the efforts of his life to the principle that it requires an educated and informed public to give character and meaning to society. The College of Medicine is an expression of this principle in action. Under his leadership the public became involved in providing the private funds initially required for the construction of this first building of the College of Medicine."

In any region the power grid, often called the Establishment, is composed of various parts. At the center are those individuals who hold the power. They may include legislators, bankers, farmers, and industrialists; and they are usually found at the power base, which in Arizona is the Salt River Valley. Agencies for channeling power are the publishers, of whom Arizona's greatest were Bill Mathews and Gene Pulliam. Throughout the grid are those who aid legislators and agencies in applying the power. They are the lobbyists.

There is another figure who can play a key role in the use of power for social good. He is the educator. Arizona has produced a major example. He is Richard Anderson Harvill, for twenty years the president of the University of Arizona. In the time of his leadership he saw the school rise from the upper limits of mediocrity to the threshold of excellence; and in the fields of anthropology-archaeology and astronomy-optical sciences to excellence itself. The standards of scholarship which led to the recognition of the Tucson campus as the only accreditable location for the medical school were the result of Harvill's two decades of upgrading of faculty appointments and student admission requirements. In addition to support from his predecessor, the legal scholar Byron McCormick, his strongest aids in this scholarly campaign were vice-presidents Robert L. Nugent and David A. Patrick; dean of Liberal Arts, Francis O. Roy; and the dean of the Graduate College, Herbert D. Rhodes.

It is not enough that an educator possess charm and political sagacity such as that of President Grady Gammage, who long held sway over the Tempe campus and saw it gain university rank. President Rufus B. von KleinSmid of the University of Southern California (and of the University of Arizona from 1914 to 1921) also had this quality. Yet unless an educator succeeds in raising the intellectual standards of his institution, his labors will be for naught when national ratings are applied. Such a combination of personal leadership and institutional quality gained under Harvill resulted in the Tucson campus's becoming the major university in the Southwest between the University of Texas and UCLA.

Harvill came to the university in 1934 as a young instructor in Economics. Born on a Tennessee farm, one of twelve children, reared in Mississippi and schooled there and in the North, he had the common voice that enabled him to speak to all segments of Arizona's society from capital to crossroads. He was a Southern gentleman in ordinary discourse, and yet when necessary his words could blister or flay.

Harvill won the respect of businessmen, ranchers, and legislators throughout Arizona when during World War II he served as price administrator in the Office of Price Administration—the OPA. After returning to the university, he rose through professorship and deanships to his appointment in 1951 as president. For two decades he provided the kind of leadership that President Robert Gordon Sproul gave the University of California for an even longer time. His success came from the energy, imagination, integrity, and courage with which he worked with students and faculty, regents and legislators, alumni and citizenry. Although a Democrat, his governance of the university was nonpartisan. He was respected by the politicians of both parties.

No one understood the power grid better than Harvill. Thus his range was wider than Tucson and the southern counties. His support was statewide and from ranchers, bankers, businessmen, and politicians—such leading Arizonans as Giss of Yuma, Fritz of Clifton, Haseltine of Prescott, the Babbitts of Flagstaff, Morris of Globe, the Udalls of St. Johns, and Bimson, Laney, and Pulliam of the Salt River Valley.

From State Librarian Marguerite Cooley I gained insight into Harvill's ways. "When there was a budget hearing," she recalled, "Dr. Harvill would arrive early, come in and say good morning; then in the reading room he would spread his papers out on the table and put them in order and relax for a few minutes. At hearings, which I sometimes attended, he would speak without looking at his material. I never heard him raise his voice—that soft Southern voice of his. He always had the answers. My goodness, he was convincing!"

Also effective as a statewide university spokesman was Vice President Marvin D. Johnson. Born in Willcox of a ranching family and married to a member of the old Pacheco family, "Swede" Johnson looked and walked as though he had just swung out of the saddle. Harvill knew the value of a balanced staff in a state not far removed from the frontier.

Fortunately for the university, Harvill and Mathews proved compatible, although at times they struck fire from each other. There are weather reports of the blue air that sometimes crackled around these two tough *hombres*. What always brought them back together was their devotion to public education.

When in 1971 Harvill relinquished his office to John Paul Schaefer, the strong son of a German immigrant steelworker, he knew the wisdom of the regents' choice, for it was he who had brought the young chemist to the university from Caltech in 1960 and set him on the administrative road that led from departmental chairmanship through deanship to the presidency. In the first five years of his tenure Schaefer has quickened the drive toward excellence begun by his predecessor.

Regardless of their party, Arizonans are conservative. Tucsonans especially so. The city's present Democratic majority is not necessarily liberal and is never radical. Tucson has not known the kind of postwar immigration that flooded the Salt River Valley to form a new conservative middle class. Through the years Tucson's non-voting "Snowbirds" flew in for the winter and flew out again before summer. Only the "old families" stayed, sweating it out with swamp coolers and even cruder home-made devices before modern air conditioning made the heat bearable. They were content with the town as it was—a tourist and health and trading center which grew around the campus. The problems and profits of industry were gladly left to Phoenix. Even though the power kept flowing into the Salt River Valley, Tucsonans seemed not unduly concerned. The Douglases' Southern Arizona Bank (which in 1975 was absorbed by the Phoenix-based, California-owned First National Bank of Arizona) never sought to rival the Bimson bank, which opened its first Tucson branch in 1936.

Tucson could have had light industry. When Motorola looked for an Arizona site, Tucson was its first choice. The Old Pueblo declined to be chosen, and the huge facility went to the Valley of the Sun, where today its plants are models of landscaped planning. And Tucson today? Except for the Hughes plant it is still without major industry. Instead it has major sprawl.

And so Tucson continues to patronize Phoenix even as San Francisco scorns Los Angeles, the Queen of the Cow Counties. Was Tucson not the Ancient and Honorable Old Pueblo? When the *Arizona Republic* taunted the southern city with a sarcastic feature called "Tucson . . . Peerless, Proud, Preposterous," the *Tucson Daily Citizen* reprinted it in full with the laconic comment, "As Others See Us." [8]

Tucson society grouped itself by when its members or their progenitors had arrived in state or territory. Each group had its own definition of "pioneer." Back in 1884 when Poston sounded the call for old-timers to come together in the organization that was originally called the Society of Arizona Pioneers and later became the Arizona Pioneers' Historical Society, he insisted that the only true pioneer was one who had arrived in Arizona before the centennial of 1876. As a Unionist among Confederate sympathizers, he was of the minority, and so off he went to Phoenix and there organized another society with himself as president.

Today the Arizona Historical Society ("Pioneer" has been dropped from the name) is still headquartered in Tucson and now acknowledges Poston as its founder. It has different categories of membership; the most esteemed is for those who came before statehood. Those who arrived at least thirty years ago can still be pioneers of lesser rank.

This distinction was observed from the first as we read in George Hand's diary of December 29, 1886. When serving as the doorman at an evening affair given by the Society, he refused to admit those who did not qualify according to the by-laws, i.e., who had arrived after the railroad. The next day he reported hard feelings by those whom he had turned away. Still, he declared, as long as he was the doorman, the by-laws were going to be enforced.

And so the Old Pueblo went its lazy provincial way—until refrigeration opened Pandora's Box. From it there emerged a swarm of land developers. A few farsighted ones had already acquired the choice Catalina foothills. Today's spokesmen for controlled growth regret the city's failure to preserve the *bajada*

8. "Tucson . . . Peerless, Proud, Preposterous" *Arizona Republic,* reprinted in *Tucson Daily Citizen* 6 June 1972.

as a green belt. A referendum in 1974 authorized the county supervisors to buy acreage for open space and parks.

Tucson also failed to follow that older pueblo of Santa Fe which limited the height of its buildings, including the state capitol, to three stories and also favored the so-called native architecture, actually a hybrid of Pueblo Indian and Mexican. The city's newest structures including the massive Arizona Medical Center could as well be in Des Moines, Dallas, or Honolulu. Tucson's misnamed Speedway is a classic example of urban ugliness.

Some twenty miles up the Santa Cruz toward Mexico lies Green Valley, the state's most attractive retirement community. Tucson is now ringed by missile sites and also by mobile homes in what some call aluminum ghettoes. When the monsoons arrive, these often unsecured abodes are sometimes lofted and blown apart.

Tucson's finest attractions lie beyond the city's limits. There is the cool summit of Kitt Peak where observatories mingle with native oaks and the picnic area is remote and peaceful. Nearer by is the Arizona Sonora Desert Museum, a living monument to the philanthropy of Arthur Pack and other generous supporters, as well as to the planning of William H. Carr and the directorship of William Woodin and Mervin Larsen. Throughout his final years this biological oasis was beloved of Joseph Wood Krutch.

Madera Canyon in the Santa Ritas is a sanctuary for people as well as birds. The Saguaro National Monuments—protected areas of saguaro cactus—to the west and east of the city are like no other landscape on earth. Redington Pass leads between the Santa Catalinas and the Rincon mountains to the valley of the San Pedro. Tucsonans thus find it easy to escape the pressures of the city.

Now, as it enters its third century, the Old Pueblo is suffering from growing pains. City council, county supervisors, and boards of education are split by controversy in the nevertheless healthy democratic process. More people mean more problems. From *ranchería* to pueblo, frontier outpost, village, and town and still not a real city, Tucson aspires to a million inhabitants by the turn of the century. Thus it seems fated to become another metropolis, choked by traffic and smothered by dusty fumes, a city such as those, east and west, from which people fled in search of a quieter, cleaner place to live. They came to Tucson as to oasis and sanctuary. Although it is still a fair and healthful place to live and work and play, uncontrolled growth will transform it. Will this be soon? Reader, turn back to the lines of Auden which ended the last chapter.

9

A Look at the Arts

I N a state as rich as Arizona in landscape and lore, it is not astonishing to find that its creative arts are also rich and varied. Histories need to be written which will trace their development from the earliest times of Indian pottery, basketry, weaving, and talismanic sculpture and jewelry. Aboriginal influences on contemporary arts and crafts are also worth study. Still another fruitful subject is the role of Fred Harvey whose Santa Fe services pioneered the collection and display of Indian arts. He also sponsored the Indian Detours initiated by Erna Fergusson whereby passengers left the railroad at Lamy, New Mexico, and after visiting the pueblos by bus, rejoined the train farther along the line at Gallup, Winslow, or Williams. The Southern Pacific had a similar Apache Trail detour.

Yet to be studied are the ways in which writers of Western romances have found uses for early diaries, memoirs, and reports of explorations. Arizona is rich in historic sources for literature and art. Museums and libraries from Flagstaff to Dragoon invite research into these source materials. Arizona, New Mexico, and the wider Southwest await a writer who will see the region as Van Wyck Brooks saw the Northeast when he wrote *The Flowering of New England*. There has also been a flowering of the Southwest.

As the region has been conquered and tranquilized, thus affording the leisure that the arts require, there has occurred a quickening of creativity in Arizona. Here in this chapter are indicated only a few characteristic responses to the land.

The land itself has been a major factor in determining the popular view of Arizona. In their reaction to it, writers, artists, and photographers have fashioned a universal image of the state—for example, artist Frederic Remington, writer Zane Grey, and the magazine *Arizona Highways*—so that to people elsewhere Arizona is cavalry soldiers and cowboys, the Grand Canyon and the Painted Desert, saguaros at sunset, Indian dances and Anglo rodeos, badmen, sheriffs, and shoot-outs.

Even Arizonans, particularly those more recent arrivals whose orbits revolve around the links and pools of Phoenix, Scottsdale, and Sun City, Tucson and Green Valley, are wedded to these misconceptions. Arizona's historic heritage, the grandeurs and miseries of its exploration and colonization, strife and pacification, and the heroes from Kino, Cooke, and Mangas to Poston, Powell, and Hunt, as well as the engineers of dams and waterways and other builders—this nobler Arizona is mostly unknown to those whose vision is that of the mass media.

Who struck the first Arizona clichés? Remington was an early artificer with his sketches of the Apache campaigns for the national magazines. He was a good reporter who saw clearly and drew truly, and then returned to the New York studio where his heart lay. J. Ross Browne never gained a comparable audience. He was too honest. His sardonic view of himself in such drawings as "The Fine Arts in Arizona" resulted in a blend of humor and realism that did not create stereotypes.

Augustus Thomas created another popular view of the state. His romantic turn-of-the-century stage hit, *Arizona,* was a pastiche of soldiers, cowboys, and virtuous womanhood, which transpired where Hooker's Rancho Sierra Bonita met the military post of Fort Grant. The play proved ephemeral. It lacked roots in the realities of Arizona.

On the contrary, Zane Grey's early and best novels—*The Heritage of the Desert, Riders of the Purple Sage* and its sequel *The Rainbow Trail*—are read to this day. Their characters inhabit a land realer than they are.

This sense of geographical reality came from the impact of Arizona on Zane Grey at that most sensitive and responsive of all times—his honeymoon. He brought his bride to the Grand Canyon in 1906, then returned alone to write the story of Buffalo Jones and his ranch on the North Rim where he was crossing Galway cattle with bison. With his *The Last of the Plainsmen* this most successful and influential of all Western writers began a lucrative romance with Arizona.

When Zane Grey packed into the canyonlands with a party of Mormons, the necessary elements were there to catalyze his gifts as a storyteller. The Grand Canyon's color and grinding power, the mysterious Anasazi ruins at Betatakin and Keet Seel, and the majesty of the Rainbow Bridge, which he was one of the earliest Anglos to visit, gave his novels what reality they achieved.

Grey's reaction to polygamy was ambivalent. At the same time that his newly proven virility was aroused by the Mormons' sexual plenty, his Victorian morality was shocked. The latter triumphed. The Mormons were his best villains.

Until *Riders of the Purple Sage* rocketed Grey into orbit, the finest of the Western clichés was in *The Virginian* when in a poker game Owen Wister's hero said to the bully who had bad-mouthed him, "When you call me that, *smile.*" And thus it remained until Lassiter rode onto the scene. When that noble gunman, Jane, and little Fay are fleeing from Tull's Mormons and have gained the threshold of the hidden valley where safety lies only if Lassiter rolls the balancing rock that will seal them in and destroy their pursuers—then comes that supreme moment when the woman cries, "Roll the stone, Lassiter, I love you!"

Although sex is not lacking in Zane Grey's stories, its presence is only implicit, and is the more exciting in being left to the reader to imagine its consummation.

Grey wrote dozens more Western romances of declining literary merit. Popular taste is undiscriminating. His ability to tell a swift tale won him worldwide readership and in one year an income of $650,000. His chromatic Arizona and cardboard characters created a distorted view of the land. Yet as the critic T. K. Whipple perceived in *Study Out the Land,* Grey's work possesses a mythic quality akin to the sagas of Beowulf. His success was no accident.

Grey was followed to the Navajo lands by Oliver La Farge, a Harvard student who came in the early 1920s as pick-and-shovel man on a "dig" in the Anasazi ruins at the Four Corners. The land seized this young man as it did Zane Grey. He returned for several summers to live the life and learn the language of the Navajos.

After his graduation, his career was diverted to the Mayan excavations of Central America being conducted by Tulane University. He then settled in New Orleans to complete his Harvard M.A. thesis on Navajo ceremonialism. He looked back sorrowfully on what he believed to be The People's lost way of life, destroyed by the railroad, the automobile, and the white man's bureaucracy. In elegiac mood La Farge wrote his first novel— *Laughing Boy.*

It was a triumph. The presence on the Pulitzer jury of Western writers Mary Austin and Owen Wister ensured its winning the award. With the added prestige of its being the Literary Guild's selection, its sales soared and have never descended. Thus was heralded a new era of fiction about the Indians.

Although he wrote a dozen more books and became a leader in the movement for Indian rights, Oliver La Farge never surpassed the achievement of his first book. For the rest of his life it hung like the albatross around his neck. He became disillusioned by the decadent ways of the tribe he had romantically idealized. In a foreword to the 1962 edition of *Laughing Boy* he wrote of the Navajos:

> They are an unhappy people, sullen towards all others, unfriendly, harassed by drunkenness, their leaders at once arrogant and

touchy. Still, here and there among them you can still find the beauty, the religion, the sense of fun, you can still attend a ceremony at which no one is drunk. In the space of thirty years, however, the wholeness has gone, the people described in *Laughing Boy,* complete to itself, is gone.[1]

Laughing Boy remains *the* romantic novel of Arizona's greatest tribe. As well as a tragic love story of The People and their Anglo corrupters, it is also a triumph of poetry over scholarship. In Laughing Boy's love for Slim Girl, La Farge lightened the learning that informed his Harvard thesis with ecstatic passages such as this:

> I have been down Old Age River in the log, with sheet-lightning and rainbows and soft rain, and the gods on either side to guide me. The Eagles have put lightning snakes and sunbeams and rainbows under me; they have carried me through the hole in the sky. I have been through the little crack in the rocks with Red God and seen the homes of the Butterflies and the Mountain Sheep and the Divine Ones. I have heard the Four Singers on the Four Mountains. I mean that woman.[2]

Northern Arizona has no monopoly on the state's creative literature. There is the heartland of Gila County, and its spokesman is Ross Santee. As a youth in his native Iowa, Santee determined to be an artist. He studied at the Art Institute in Chicago and then in New York. When he failed at first, he sought solace with relatives in Globe. There, as a horse wrangler on the Bar F Bar outfit on the Apache Indian reservation, he found himself as an artist and a writer as well. By the end of his life in 1965 Ross Santee had become the laureate of the range, the peer of New Mexico's Rhodes and of Dobie, the great Texan.

As the northland inspired Zane Grey and Oliver La Farge, so did the heartland catalyze the gifts of Ross Santee. When he came to Gila County in 1915, he knew it for his inevitable

---

1. Oliver La Farge, *Laughing Boy* (Boston: Houghton Mifflin, 1929, 1962), pp. vii–ix.

2. LaFarge, *Laughing Boy,* p. 158.

home. Here is how he saw it: ". . . the great mesas, shimmering in the sun. Beyond them the ranges rolled and pitched as far as the eyes could see. I had never seen such color. But it was the country itself that did something to me." [3] What that country did to Ross Santee was art and literature, no less.

A year after his arrival in Arizona Santee began to draw again, first with a burnt match on his chaps—drew what he had come to know and to love, the land and the remuda he wrangled. He was also moved to write—tales of the top hands and wranglers and their horses, and of the San Carlos and Whiteriver Apaches by whom he was accepted. The New York that had spurned his arty drawings now hailed his new work as it appeared in such books as *Men and Horses, Cowboy, Lost Pony Tracks,* and *Apache Land.* "Too bad more artists don't go the Arizona," George Bellows said of Ross Santee. "Maybe they'd learn to draw." [4]

Santee's work is deceptively simple. With a few lines of black on white he suggests the immensity of distance and the emptiness of sky that are the hallmarks of Arizona as much as the colors of the Painted Desert and Monument Valley. Although Santee drew hundreds of horses, no two are alike. His work is Arizona classically understated. As Grey and La Farge depict a romantic Arizona, so is Santee the master of a laconic realism. Meaningless violence is absent from his work. The only instance of gunplay occurs when the foreman of the outfit lies in his bunk and picks flies off the ceiling with his .38. I predict that Ross Santee will be read long after Boot Hill has been leveled.

Among these books there is a supreme masterpiece of creative literature. It is the novel *Apache* by Will Levington Comfort, the unheralded next-to-last of his many works. Whereas Grey, La Farge, and Santee wrote about a land they knew and

3. Ross Santee, *Lost Pony Tracks* (New York: Scribner, 1953), p. 9.

4. Ross Santee, "Advice Is All Right If You Don't Take Too Much of It," *American Magazine,* June 1928.

lives they had witnessed or lived, Comfort knew Arizona only briefly and at the end of a life spent elsewhere. In the course of a long writing career he had mastered his craft, and in an intense life as a war correspondent and cult founder, he had gained insight and compassion; so that when he came to the domain of Cochise and Mangas, their land claimed him even as Navajoland and the Gila range did his literary precursors.

Chance brought him to Arizona. He first came to help steady an alcoholic son who was working on the Bisbee newspaper. While passing through Tombstone "on its high mesquite mesa" en route to Brewery Gulch, Comfort discovered in the files of the *Epitaph* a lucrative article for the *Saturday Evening Post*. Then as he read more, the journalist was replaced by the novelist. Here is how he told it: "The red, glistening thread of the Apache wove constantly through the gray fabric of pioneer talk, far more interesting than the attempt to put the old town back." [5] In the tragedy of Mangas Coloradas, the rimrock Mimbreño chieftain delivered to his executioners by Jack Swilling, Will Comfort found the theme that fired his imagination to incandescence.

Research in field and library documented, and Comfort's mystical identification with Mangas exalted this strange novel. Although savage, *Apache* is not sordid; its tragedy is not tearful. *Apache* is an austere tribute to a leader lost, a people gone. In some mysterious way Comfort wrote as an Apache might have written. As a work of art it transcends that other lament, *Laughing Boy*.

In writing *Apache* Comfort was consumed. Publication in 1931 was followed by his death. He died knowing that he had written a masterpiece. This is a judgment shared by literary critics and ethnologists. It was his good fortune to go at his peak, and, unlike Grey and La Farge, be spared a long decline of creative power.

5. James V. Mink, "The Making of a Southwest Novel," *Manuscripts* 9:3, (Summer 1957).

Arizona has not been kind to its poets. Only an epic bard could do justice to the forms and colors and the sagas of bloodshed, suffering, and heroism that have marked the land. No poet has come to Arizona as Robinson Jeffers came to California.

And yet Arizona has known one who, if not a great poet, was a noble woman and a great Arizonan. Her name was Sharlot Hall, and she came to Yavapai County from Kansas in 1882 as a girl of twelve with her parents and a party of emigrants. "I rode into Prescott on a long-legged, dapple-gray mare who had just left her footprints on the full length of the Santa Fe trail. We had been three months coming—three winter months with covered wagons and a caravan of loose horses—like Abraham and his family seeking new grazing grounds." [6]

They settled on Lynx Creek twelve miles southeast of town, and there on Orchard Ranch she helped her father and mother work the land. Although she received little schooling, she became a writer, first on Charles F. Lummis's magazine, *Land of Sunshine,* where she served as contributing editor for Arizona. When the magazine's name was changed to *Out West,* she wrote the title poem. With an illustration by another youthful contributor, Maynard Dixon, the poem was made into a broadside and sent throughout the land. Hall and Dixon represented the new talent Lummis enlisted to help make his magazine the peer of California's *Overland Monthly.*

In 1905 President Roosevelt's endorsement of Senator Beveridge's proposal that Arizona and New Mexico be admitted as a single state aroused Sharlot Hall's indignation. She wrote an impassioned poem marked by such lines as

We will wait outside your sullen door till the stars
    that ye wear grow dim
As the pale dawn-stars that swim and fade o'er our
    mighty Cañon's rim,

6. *Sharlot Hall on the Arizona Strip,* edited by C. Gregory Crampton (Flagstaff: Northland Press, 1975), p. 2.

We will lift no hand for the bays ye wear, nor covet
   your robes of state—
But ah! By the skies above us we will shame ye while we wait.[7]

Her account of the poem's writing bears quoting:

> I was then gathering material for a special Arizona Statehood
> number of the *Out West Magazine*. I had been through the snow-
> covered forests around Flagstaff and was threatened with pneumo-
> nia from exposure. Coming by train from Flagstaff to the ranch, I
> got the papers and read the message. I grew more and more indig-
> nant as I read, and after reaching the ranch I asked my mother,
> who thought I was coming down with pneumonia, to let me have a
> fire in the sitting room and have the family go to bed and let me
> alone. I finished the poem by eleven o'clock that night, and the
> anger had entirely cured the cold.[8]

Governor Kibbey had the poem printed as a broadside and
placed on the desk of every member of Congress. Territorial
Delegate Smith read it aloud on the floor of the House. It helped
bring about the referendum in which Arizona rejected Roosevelt's proposal.

In 1909 Sharlot Hall was named territorial historian. During
the next three years she traveled throughout Arizona to every
county but Santa Cruz, gathering historical data and pioneer
lore. Because of the Mexican Revolution of 1910 she was unable to visit the little border county. When Utah sought to annex
the land isolated by the Grand Canyon and known as the Arizona Strip, she hired a guide and wagon and went on an arduous
reconnaissance of the remote land. Her articles in a Phoenix
magazine helped repulse the Mormon advance.[9]

A volume of her verse was published in 1910 with the title
Cactus and Pine, and was followed ten years after her death in
1943 by *Poems of a Ranchwoman.*

7. Sharlot Hall, *Cactus and Pine,* second edition (Phoenix: Arizona Republican,
1924), pp. 107–108.

8. Hall, *Cactus and Pine,* p. 106.

9. Crampton, *Sharlot Hall,* p. 2.

When in 1927 age, illness, and the death of her father forced Sharlot Hall to leave the ranch and move to Prescott, her love for Arizona led to the resurrection of the ruined loghouse that had been built in 1864 for the governor's mansion. She transformed it into a museum of pioneer memorabilia.

During the Depression, WPA funds were used to erect a stone building for Sharlot Hall's collection. Today it and the First Governor's House stand in the heart of the Old Capital as a shrine to a vanished Arizona.

On her swing through Arizona in writing *Our Southwest,* author Erna Fergusson called on Sharlot Hall in her apartment at the back of the museum. She admired her literary colleague as a woman "grounded in the realism I found so inspiring. By living close to it she gathered her sense of the Southwest which she expressed later in poetry. *Cactus and Pine* was a good title for her. Thorny cactus makes marvelous beauty out of its struggle for existence, and pines are invariably straight and true." [10]

If Arizona's grandeur has daunted its poets, what of its painters? The land's brilliant forms thwart those who would capture them in paint. If copies are what is sought, then color photographs are truer to life. In this painter's paradise nearly every town has a gallery where Western oils and watercolors are seen and sold. There have been notable collectors including Walter Bimson, Lewis Douglas, and James S. Douglas, whose banks served as galleries in which to hang their pictures. [11] Read Mullan, the Phoenix auto dealer, also has a superb collection.

"What is Art?" asked the jesting aesthete and would not stay for an answer. The common man's answer satisfies most people: "I may not know what Art is, but I know what I like."

At the risk of being bundled in wet rawhide and left in the

10. Erna Fergusson, *Our Southwest* (New York: Alfred A. Knopf, 1940), pp. 184–188.

11. *The West and Walter Bimson* (Tucson: University of Arizona Museum of Art, 1971). Southern Arizona Bank, Tucson, *A Collection of Western Art* (1973) [brochure].

sun, I here give my answer to both aesthete and commoner: *Art is seeing with inner and outer vision so that what is rendered on canvas, though not literal, is recognizable.* Thus are eliminated both copies and distortions.

I shall ignore the many good Arizona painters and focus on a single great one—great in the sense that during his long creative life, in looking both inwardly and outwardly, he saw Arizona with double vision. He was also never content to go on repeating his successes.

This painter's full name was Lafayette Maynard Dixon. He was born in 1875 in California's San Joaquin Valley at Fresno of old Virginia stock. Like Ross Santee, he knew from boyhood that he would be an artist. When he sent sketches to the great Remington, the encouragement received served him the rest of his life. His first success came as a newspaper artist in San Francisco. It was Lummis, that unfailing perceiver of genius, who, after publishing Dixon's work in the new magazine, sent the young artist across the Colorado to larger scenes. In Prescott Dixon hobnobbed with Sharlot Hall's father.

The turn of the century found him drawing Indians and horses at Ganado where he was befriended by the trader Lorenzo Hubbell. The drawings made by Dixon on this and other early trips to Arizona and Utah were discovered after his death and edited by Don Perceval for the Northland Press as *A Maynard Dixon Sketchbook*. They show his mastery of sketching from life urged by Remington in his response to the boy's drawings.

When Dixon returned to San Francisco, he took with him Navajo blankets on consignment from Hubbell, and when the earthquake and fire of 1906 destroyed his studio, it was the blankets that he saved rather than his own paintings. Their top price then was $25.

Dixon's first public work was painted in 1909 for the new Southern Pacific station in Tucson. Four lunettes for the high windows of the waiting room represented the typical Arizonan characters of Cattleman, Apache, Prospector, and Irrigator. The three that survived neglect were kept in Arizona by the generosity of Clay Lockett, and may be seen at the Arizona Historical Society in Tucson.

Dixon found it necessary to move to New York in order to make a living as an artist. There he became an illustrator of magazines and books, including the Hopalong Cassidy stories. Yet he was not happy. Editors wanted only the clichés of the Far West. "I am being paid to lie about the West," he wrote to Lummis, "the country I know and care about. I'm going back home where I can do honest work." [12] So he returned to San Francisco and in time became a successful muralist, with commissions to decorate banks, libraries, hotels, restaurants, steamships, and post offices. To the dining room of the Arizona Biltmore in Phoenix he contributed several romantic panels of Indians. During the Depression he painted a stark series on the suffering he saw.

In 1939 Dixon moved to Tucson for relief from asthma and there (with summers in Utah) he worked until his death in 1946. From the north window of his studio on Prince Road he looked on the Santa Catalinas, and he repeatedly painted that range in changing light and color, so that in his final work it occupies a place akin to that of Mont St. Victoire in the work of Cézanne.

As Dixon aged, his vision of Arizona grew bolder and more geometric and showed kinship with Indian art forms. An essential element of his greatness is that his art never stopped growing. He came to see earth and sky ever more impressionistically. The critic Arthur Millier wrote of Maynard Dixon:

> His paintings show us the desert lands so convincingly that people
> often think they have seen in nature exactly what they see in one
> of his pictures. This is seldom possible, for he generally rearranges
> the elements of the scene before him to make a rhythmical and
> harmonious composition. What actually occurs in such cases is
> that he opens our eyes to the country. Where many have looked,
> he is one of the few who have really seen. His vision of the West

12. Wesley Burnside, *Maynard Dixon, Artist of the West* (Provo: Brigham Young University Press, 1974), p. 55.

is so true that we have come to see the region through the forms and colors of his paintings. Thus great artists teach us to see nature.[13]

Arizona has yet to recognize its greatest painter with any major collection of his work. Utah has proved more perceptive. Brigham Young University in Provo owns a distinguished representation of Dixon's paintings and sketches, including the powerful Depression series, and has published a sumptuous monograph thereon.[14]

It is fitting that Dixon's ashes were buried in Utah at Mt. Carmel where he spent his last summers. He wrote his own epitaph:

> At last
> I shall give myself to the desert again,
> that I, in its golden dust,
> may be blown from a barren peak
> broadcast over the sun-lands
>
> If you should desire some news of me,
> go ask the little horned toad whose home is the dust,
> or seek it among the fragrant sage,
> or question the mountain juniper,
> and, by their silence,
> they will truly inform you.[15]

In olden times an Arizonan packed a pistol. Today he carries a camera. No proper person would be seen without a Nikon. And there is the sad story of the tourist who fell into Lake Havasu and was dragged to the bottom by the cameras he was wearing.

A century ago John K. Hillers rode the Colorado with Powell and photographed "all the best scenery." The Kolb brothers were among the early photographers of the Grand Canyon. Their studio on the South Rim is a museum of memorabilia including the boat in which they first ran the river.

13. Arthur Millier, *Maynard Dixon, Painter of the West* (Tucson: 1945), p. 2.

14. Burnside, *Artist of the West.*

15. Millier, *Painter of the West,* p. 4.

Among Charles Lummis's many accomplishments was photography. He was active in the 1890s, although most of his field work was in New Mexico. Before the turn of the century, A. C. Vroman, the Pasadena bookseller, photographed the Hopis. The discovery of his lost negatives led to the publication of two books of his Arizona prints.

Color photography reached its apotheosis in *Arizona Highways,* originally a dull house organ, which Raymond Carlson transformed and made famous. When a poll was recently taken of the reasons why immigrants had come to Arizona, one in three replied that it was the magazine that had brought them.

By the use of color shots *Arizona Highways* created a stereotype by which Arizona appears only beautiful. Neither in picture nor in text is it shown other than majestic, idyllic, and untroubled. Duststorms, floods, slag heaps, smelter pollution, urban smog, and slums have no place in its pages. It is a dazzling display of Boosterism envied by the other Western states also hungry for the tourist dollar.

Raymond Carlson grew up in Globe as still another creative son of Gila County, and was educated at Stanford, where he earned a Phi Beta Kappa key. With political shrewdness he ruled as an absolute editor for thirty-three years, during which he increased the magazine's circulation to the hundreds of thousands. Comparatively few subscribers were in Arizona. The colorful periodical was for export.

Carlson had flair. He recognized the genius of Ross Santee. During the Depression when Santee directed the Federal Writers Project, which produced the state guide, Carlson found the project's writers a source of copy. He also reproduced the work of contemporary painters, including Maynard Dixon, and gathered their magazine appearances in *A Gallery of Western Painting.* Ted De Grazia, who became Arizona's most popular painter, was discovered by Carlson in the early years when Ted was hardly more than the ambitious son of a Morenci miner.

Arizona Highways founded its fame on the work of the West's finest photographers including Ansel Adams, Josef

Muench and later his son David, Ray Manley, Darwin Van Campen, Chuck Abbott, Esther Henderson, Willis Peterson, and Arthur Dailey, the greatest photographer of the remuda. Carlson's showcase glorified a radiant land of red rocks, autumn colors, and the flowers that carpet the desert—a far piece from our dry and wrinkled land!

When Carlson retired in 1971, he was succeeded by his protegé, Joseph Stacey, who inaugurated a new era in the magazine's history with a series of stunning issues on Arizona's native crafts, antique and modern, including jewelry, pottery, weaving, and basketry. The magazine is now edited by Tom Cooper.

Is this all I have to say about the arts in Arizona? Nothing about music and dance and architecture? Mariachi masses? Indian ceremonials? Frank Lloyd Wright and Taliesin West, Paolo Soleri and his Arizona underground, or about Benny Gonzalez's charming public library buildings in Wickenburg, Phoenix, Scottsdale, Mesa, and Nogales?

All of them and more I leave to other writers, other books, while I go on to more urgent matters, to at least a mention of some of the problems that trouble us and to the question What lies beyond the bicentennial?

10

Beyond the Bicentennial

WHEN we come to ask what lies beyond the bicentennial, we have reached the hardest part of this brief history. If we believe that we are because of what we were and will be what we have been, then it should be possible to read the future. If time is a continuum—that is, a thing whose parts cannot be separately discerned or isolated—then we have only to struggle out on the bank of the time-stream and observe our history as a long pageant without beginning, middle, or end. Then we could know what lies beyond the bicentennial.

A history based on the past and present is easy to write compared to a history that seeks also to include the future. Yet I believe that the future is there if we could only manage to perceive it. All through history there have been seers able to pierce the curtain that veils the future. Theirs is a dubious power. Too much revelation of the future might mean paralysis, as the prospect proved too much for us to contemplate.

In olden times man went to the Delphic oracle. When I went to the Arizona oracle with questions about the future, there was no answer. The wind was strong that day, the sky was obscured. Hearing and seeing were difficult. I never went back. The way is long and hard and one must carry his own water, there on the far side of Baboquívari.

And so when I ask what lies beyond 1976, I must be my own

oracle. There is no use searching the state for answers. I tried that. Although many know the problems, few know the answers, especially practical ones. Perhaps there are none. Maybe we should proceed from the answers to the questions. Confusing, isn't it? If I did not believe in the continuum of time, I would despair.

Yet I do believe and am confident that the answers are there, only waiting for us to hear them, if—if—if what? If I had the extra sense of prophet, poet, or scientist, then I could wrap it all up—past, present, and future—in this little package called Book.

I am not the first to embrace a mystical concept of time. The desert has always favored insight. There was John the Baptist, whose name was borne by Anza. The immensity of land and sky, the clarity of days and nights, have heightened the perceptions of desert dwellers. At the turn of our century the writer John Van Dyke came for health, and when he regained it, he left his thanks in *The Desert*. Then the philosopher-naturalist Joseph Wood Krutch spent the last twenty years of his life giving voice to the desert. Their books are basic for an understanding of this austere land.

What are some of our problems? The greatest is, as I see it, peculiarly Arizonan, that of a rising flood of people into a land naturally unsuited to large numbers of people. They do not adapt to this land; they have adapted it to them. I began by calling it a great dry and wrinkled land, a land of mountains and deserts, meager rainfall and dwindling rivers. It is also a land of delicate interconnectedness and of a fragile ecology. By our technology we have vanquished heat and drought and thus offered to millions a way of comfortable and leisurely life. We call it the Arizona lifestyle and advertise it throughout the world as an invitation to better living. No wonder that Arizona is one of the fastest growing states.

To what end? To disaster, some say. To greater prosperity and happiness, say others. If we go to the past, there is only one answer: *All cultures die.* Some live longer than others; none lives forever. On the ruins of the Hohokam the people of the Salt River Valley work and play in the sun, there in the Valley of the Sun. Meanwhile the risen Phoenix soars above the Vale of Tempe.

Yet our culture cannot escape its fate, which is at last to die, nor can we foresee how and when it will come. Perhaps imperceptibly. We know that the rock of Roosevelt Dam will survive the rammed earth of Casa Grande, although there may not be any water behind the dam. Built as it is of steel and concrete, Tucson's community center will survive the adobes of San Xavier, although it may finally be inhabited only by birds and bats.

If to remain habitable for commerce and pleasure, Arizona must have cooled air, then its life span is shorter, for the fossil fuel sources of energy to cool the air are running out. Coal, gas, water—all are in falling reserves. Solar energy and atomic power are uncertain, costly sources. Modern Arizona's cool, mobile, and expansive way of life can be projected to a fairly precise terminal date. That it may be in centuries rather than decades offers slight cause for optimism.

I would not have the reader believe me a Jeremiah. I am really a cheerful person. Arizona's today, even her tomorrow, is enchanting. It is the day after tomorrow that troubles me. I am convinced of two things that are complementary: It is a wonderful time to live in Arizona, and it is a time that will end. Did not Shakespeare write

> But thought's the slave of life, and life time's fool,
> And time, that takes survey of all the world,
> Must have a stop.[1]

How and when our time will stop we know not, any more than we know how and when that of the Anasazi and the Hohokam stopped. Barring natural cataclysm or atomic holocaust, man will probably continue to live in Arizona and adapt, as our predecessors have done, to a hostile environment. Although our

1. *King Henry IV*, Part I, act 5, scene 4.

skills have made it into an earthly paradise, it is still an arid land.

Turn off the sprinklers in summer and the golf courses will revert to desert. Cut the power and Arizonans will swelter. This paradise is ours by God's grace, man's ingenuity—and a few wires and pumps.

If we have the will, our comparatively minor problems are solvable. There is the problem of our concern for each other, of how the fortunate help the unfortunate and the way the dominant whites treat their fellow Arizonans whose skins are darker. There is the problem of too many people living in too small a place. Their autos dirty the air and yet without them, people could not live as they do in unrestricted mobility. Off-road vehicles may be heaven for their drivers, but they are hell on earth. When cultivation breaks the desert fabric, the windblown dust darkens the sky. As a result of public pressures the emissions from copper smelters are slowly being made cleaner. Even without air conditioning man could go on living in Arizona as he once did, although there would be fewer who would stay to sweat it out behind open doors and windows hung with wet sacks. There are ways of building for coolness that do not require the consumption of energy. Those who could take the heat would stay. Adaptation of man to the land and not of the land to man would be necessary.

Civilization advances in Arizona as frontier permissiveness recedes. Needed is action to outlaw the land frauds that have cost people millions of dollars. It is not as much a question of new laws as it is of enforcing old laws. Pumping of groundwater will be regulated, as the people insist that Arizona's natural resources belong to them and not to the privileged and often absent few. Arizona's archaic water laws need modernizing. Millions more immigrants will mean that this land of the least possible government, of which Barry Goldwater is the champion, will increasingly resemble its sister states of the Union. We are too intricately joined as a nation to leave government solely in local hands. What worked in an expanding society no longer works when society becomes more rigid. As the information and entertainment media continue to standardize the mores of the country, Arizona will be the last to conform. While the rest of the country tinkers with time, Arizona goes on living by the sun.

And so I end where I began, with a loving look at this great land that has always managed to live with itself. Plants and animals, upland and desert creatures, and the native peoples will go on living here world (nearly) without end. As far back as we can go on the continuum, we find people living here as hunters, gatherers, planters, and builders, eating and multiplying on foodstuffs of flesh and fruit and grain, even as we.

Now as past and present slide into future, life in Arizona is richer and easier for more and more people, creating the dangerous illusion that its very ease will ensure its survival. The truth is otherwise, and it is a hard truth, and yet if we can accept it, it is a truth that will make us free, even happy. Knowing that our future is not eternal should cause us to be more grateful for what we have, should make us humbly appreciative of the blessings our technological skills have given us.

So then let us be of good cheer, as I am, for what appears ahead, for the perception, albeit dim, that there will be life in Arizona for centuries, even millennia, to come. The procession of her possessors, including us, is a glorious one. Although it is sometimes violent and cruel, yet is it mostly peaceful and occasionally heroic; and in Arizona's dramatic theater of grand, canyoned mountains, dry lands, and chromatic skies, forever beautiful.

Let this book end with these words of a traditional Navajo blessing:

In beauty it is begun
In beauty it is finished
Go in beauty

Suggestions
for Further Reading

My choice of only thirty-four books as a reader's guide to Arizona was both arbitrary and difficult, for there is a rich and varied literature about the state. My selections continue to reveal those predilections that determined the content and nature of the preceding chapters. Not much is included on law and order, nothing on frontier violence as such, no ghost towns and lost mines, cowboy-and-Indian memoirs, little on economics and politics. The classic Arizona clichés don't interest me. Those who crave to read about them are free to choose their own books.

As I said in the preface and say again in closing, mine is merely one man's view of Arizona. I hope that it is not too unbalanced or unrecognizable. Other men, other views; other writers, different books.

Not all of the books listed are in print and purchasable from bookstores. The older books can be acquired on the secondhand market. None of them are rare and costly. All may be read in the city, county, and academic libraries with which the state is now well provided. Publishing on Arizona flourishes in Flagstaff at the Northland Press, in Tempe at the Arizona Historical Foundation, and in Tucson at the Arizona Historical Society and the University of Arizona Press. Arizona Silhouettes and Rio Grande Press have reprinted many of the classic works on the Southwest.

There are two good historical quarteries: *Arizona and the West,* edited by Harwood P. Hinton, is published by the University of Arizona Press, and *Journal of Arizona History,* edited by C. L. Sonnichsen, by the Arizona Historical Society. *Books of the Southwest* is a monthly listing, by publisher and price, of current Southwest Americana; it is edited by Donald M. Powell and Betty Rosenberg for the University of Arizona Library.

A useful work is Andrew Wallace's *Sources and Readings in Arizona History,* a compilation of articles by contemporary authorities (Tucson, 1965). An eloquent statement of Arizona's true heritage is

Bert M. Fireman's "Mostly Sweat," an address to the Arizona Pioneers' Reunion, read into the *Congressional Record* April 28, 1958, by Senator Barry Goldwater.

Although the political boundaries of Arizona separate it precisely from its neighbors, the Southwest, of which Arizona and New Mexico are the heartland, is boundaried more subtly by geography and weather and the imprint of its original possessors. And so I begin with a book that describes the Southwest in terms of the land and the movement of its peoples.

D. W. Meinig, *Southwest*. New York: Oxford University Press, 1971. Subtitled "Three Peoples in Geographical Change, 1600–1970," this 151-page book is a compact essay on the power of the land to determine history. Maps and reading list are also excellent.

Natt N. Dodge and Herbert S. Zim, *The American Southwest, A Guide to the Wide Open Spaces*. New York: Simon and Schuster, 1955. This book is remarkable for the colored lithographic illustrations by Arch and Miriam Hurford, which illuminate the pages on geography, history, archaeology, fauna, flora, and crafts.

Erna Fergusson, *Our Southwest*. New York: Alfred A. Knopf, 1940. Although obviously out of date on current things, this remains the best cultural introduction to the Southwest, learned, humane, and marked by that quality valued by Dobie above all others—*perspective*.

Howard R. Lamar, *The Far Southwest, 1846–1912, a Territorial History*. New Haven: Yale University Press, 1966; New York: W. W. Norton and Company, 1970. This outstanding work by Yale's professor of western history is solidly researched and engagingly written. It includes New Mexico, Colorado, Utah, and Arizona.

Jay J. Wagoner, *Early Arizona, Prehistory to Civil War*. Tucson: University of Arizona Press, 1975. *Arizona Territory, 1863–1912, a Political History*. Tucson: University of Arizona Press, 1970. These authoritative works by an Arizona historian are to be followed by a history of the state since its creation in 1912.

Ross Santee, editor, *Arizona, A Guide to the Grand Canyon State*. New York: Hastings House, 1940 and later revisions by Joseph Miller. This and the companion New Mexico guide are among the best of the great WPA series that came from the Depression. The book is timelessly valuable for its history, folklore, and travel itineraries. Except for the urban centers, most of Arizona remains unchanged. The reason Santee's name does not appear as editor is that the WPA officials refused to list the names of his staff. "O.K.," the tough wrangler said, "then leave mine out."

Members of the faculty of the University of Arizona, *Arizona, Its People and Resources*. Tucson: University of Arizona Press, 1960, 1972. The revised second edition constitutes an encyclopedia of the history, land, government, economy, and cultural institutions. There are many illustrations, maps, and tables, and a reading list by Donald M. Powell.

Will C. Barnes, *Arizona Place Names*. Tucson: University of Arizona Press, 1935, 1960. This first edition in paperback form is the one to travel with. The enlargement by Byrd R. Granger in 1960, published by the University of Arizona Press, is a large volume arranged by county, rather than alphabetically as is the earlier edition, thus making quick reference difficult. A new edition is in preparation that will, I hope, return to a more useful format.

Odie B. Faulk, *Arizona, a Short History*. Norman: University of Oklahoma Press, 1970. This compact, readable work is by the Southwest's most prolific historian.

Madeline F. Paré and Bert M. Fireman, *Arizona Pageant, a Short History of the 48th State*. Tempe: Arizona Historical Foundation, 1970. Written as a text for Arizona high schools, this authoritative work is a good introduction to the past and present of the state.

Edward H. Spicer, *Cycles of Conquest; the Impact of Spain, Mexico and the United States on the Indians of the Southwest, 1530–1960*. Drawings by Hazel Fontana. Tucson: University of Arizona Press, 1962. This massive work will probably remain definitive until our culture is supplanted by others.

Patricia Paylore, Ted De Grazia, and Donald M. Powell. *Kino, a Commemoration*. Tucson: Arizona Pioneers Historical Society, 1961. Issued on the 250th anniversary of Kino's death, this pamphlet includes an essay, sketches, and a bibliography.

Charles Polzer, S.J., *A Kino Guide*. Tucson: Southwestern Mission Research Center, 1972. This biography and guide to Kino's Missions and Monuments, contains a chapter on the discovery in 1966 of his grave in Magdalena, Sonora. Cartography is by Don Bufkin.

Herbert Eugene Bolton, editor and translator, *Anza's California Expeditions*, 5 vols. Reprinted, New York: Russell and Russell, 1966. This noble work combines prodigious scholarship in archives and field with sustained readability. The illustrations are from photographs taken by Bolton along the Anza route from Sonora to San Francisco.

Elliott Coues, editor and translator, *On the Trail of a Spanish Pioneer: the Diary of Francis Garcés . . . 1775–1776,* 2 vols. New York: F. P. Harper, 1900. This great work of inspiration and field studies ranks with the Bolton-Anza at the peak of Arizona historiography. Coues was an army doctor in the Southwest who trailed Garcés as Bolton did Anza.

James Ohio Pattie, *Personal Narrative,* edited by M. M. Quaife. Chicago: R. R. Donnelley, 1930. The first edition of this illiterate trapper's romantic yarn (Cincinnati: J. H. Wood, 1831) sells for thousands of dollars. This Lakeside Classics reprint is the handiest of several versions. Pattie came down the Gila in the 1820s. His garrulous narrative was written for him by Timothy Flint.

William H. Emory, *Lieutenant Emory Reports: A Reprint of . . . Notes of a Military Reconnaissance.* Abridged by Ross Calvin. Albuquerque: University of New Mexico Press, 1968. Emory was the topographical engineer who accompanied Kearny on his dash to California with dragoons, mules, and a brass howitzer. First published at Washington in 1848 as a government document (Senate Ex. Doc. 7, 30th Congress, 1st sess.), Emory's notes rank with Garcés's diary as prime Arizoniana.

J. Ross Browne, *Adventures in Apache Country.* Edited by Donald M. Powell. Tucson: University of Arizona Press, 1974. A facsimile reprint, with added material, of the original Harper edition of 1869, this is the best of all travel books on southern Arizona in the 1860s. Browne's prose and drawings are happily wed in a book humorous, sardonic, and civilized.

John G. Bourke, *On the Border with Crook.* New York: Charles Scribner's Sons, 1891. A photographic paperback edition was published in 1971 by the University of Nebraska Press.

Martha Summerhayes, *Vanished Arizona; Recollections of the Army Life of a New England Woman.* Tucson: Arizona Silhouettes, 1960. First published in 1908 (Philadelphia: J. B. Lippincott) and enlarged by the author in 1911 (Salem, Mass.: Salem Press), this classic of the Apache frontier in the 1870s has often been reprinted. This edition, which reproduces the text of 1911, with added historical notes by Ray Brandes, is the best of the modern versions.

Frank C. Lockwood, *Pioneer Portraits; Selected Vignettes.* Introduction by John Bret Harte. Tucson: University of Arizona Press,

1968. These vignettes are drawn from the author's *Pioneer Days in Arizona* (1932). The author came to the University of Arizona as an English professor, fell in love with Arizona, and became one of its most humanistic historians and biographers.

Charles S. Peterson, *Take Up Your Mission: Mormon Colonizing Along the Little Colorado River, 1870–1900*. Tucson: University of Arizona Press, 1973. This is the best account of the Mormons' contribution to the civilizing of Arizona.

Ira B. Joralemon, *Copper, the Encompassing Story of Mankind's First Metal*. Berkeley: Howell-North, 1973. Here is an enlarged edition of the author's *Romantic Copper* (New York: Appleton-Century, 1935). The Arizona story is a major part of this world-wide account.

Frank Waters, *The Colorado*. New York: Rinehart and Co., 1946. What the author sought in this volume in the Rivers of America series was the mystical spirit of the river and the area it drains, as well as the geological and human history. The struggle between Arizona and California for the river's water is treated impartially.

Frank McNitt, *The Indian Traders*. Norman: University of Oklahoma Press, 1962. An important aspect of our history has been solidly researched and engagingly written by a New England writer with a passion for the Southwest.

Don Perceval and Clay Lockett, *A Navajo Sketch Book*. Flagstaff: Northland Press, 1962. Watercolors and black-and-white drawings by Perceval and text by Lockett blend in this most beautiful of Arizona books.

Clara Lee Tanner, *Southwest Indian Craft Arts*. Tucson: University of Arizona Press, 1968. This beautiful, authoritative work by an anthropologist and art historian, was supplemented by her later *Southwest Indian Painting*.

William T. Hornaday, *Camp-Fires on Desert and Lava*. New York: Charles Scribner's Sons, 1908. This is the account of an exploring trip by a party including a botanist, zoologist, geographer, and sportsman to the little-known Pinacate volcanic desert, across the border southwest of Tucson. The elusive desert bighorn sheep was one of the objects of their quest.

Godfrey Sykes, *A Westerly Trend*. Tucson: Arizona Pioneers Historical Society, 1944. This is the autobiography of a hardy Yorkshireman who wandered west in the 1880s. Before he died in old age at Tucson, he became a cattleman, architect-engineer, hydrographer, and explorer. Sykes built the dome of the Lowell Observatory in Flagstaff, the Carnegie Desert Laboratory on Tucson's Tumamoc Hill, the road up Mt. Wilson in Pasadena, and wrote the definitive book on the delta of the Colorado. He was a man to match Arizona's mountains, rivers, and desert.

Ruth M. Underhill, *Singing for Power; the Song Magic of the Papago Indians of Southern Arizona*. Berkeley: University of California Press, 1938. Paperback reprint, Ballantine, 1973. The translations and commentary, illustrated from drawings by Indian boys, form a book of beauty and meaning.

John C. Van Dyke, *The Desert*. New York: Charles Scribner's Sons, 1901. Many subsequent reprintings. This is the first book to praise the Southwestern desert as a place of beauty, written by an Eastern art-historian who "went native" for several years at the turn of the century. It is a book of lasting influence and authority on the geology, fauna and flora, sky, and weather of the Mojave, Colorado, and Sonora deserts.

Joseph Wood Krutch, *The Desert Year*. New York: The Viking Press, 1963 and later reprints of this paperback of a work first published in 1951. After the distinguished literary figure came to Tucson in 1950, he distilled these essences from his first year of residency. His view of the arid land is that of a philosophical naturalist. This book complements Van Dyke's *The Desert* of a half century earlier.

Lawrence Clark Powell, *Southwest Classics; the Creative Literature of the Arid Lands; Essays on Books and Their Writers*. Los Angeles: Ward Ritchie Press, 1974. The authors range from Kino to Krutch and include historians, naturalists, biographers, and novelists.

Index

Abbey, Edward, 7–8

Agriculture: effect on rivers; 9, 10; of ancient Indians, 15, 16, 84; of Spanish, 20; with irrigation, 85, 89, 90, 91, 92; after World War II, 94; University of Arizona studies on, 112, 113. *See also* Irrigation

Air conditioning, 96, 119, 120, 140, 141

Ajo, open-pit mine, 53

All-American Canal, 76

Alsop, John T., 90

Alta California, 23, 24

Anglos: impact of on environment, 10, 12, 38, 80; massacres by, 26; impact of on Indian culture and religion, 35, 37, 78; predominance of in Arizona, 49–50; in Salt River Valley, 84, 89–90, 92; impact of on Tucson, 105, 106

Anza, Juan Bautista de, 23–25; mentioned, 30, 41, 74, 84, 102, 139

Apacheland. See Poston, Charles Debrille

Arid lands: Arizona among, 12; *Report on Lands of Arid Regions* (Powell), 74, 75; studies of, 81–82, 113; Newland, spokesman for, 91; effect of increased population on, 139, 140, 141

Arizona: origin of name of, 20; nicknames of, 38; problems of, 139, 141–142

—Climate and topography: mountains, 3–8; rivers, 8–10, 25; weather, 96; dependence on water, 11, 12, 83, 84, 141; ecology of, 141. *See also* Mountains; Rivers; Water; names of individual mountains, ranges, and rivers

—Settlement: ancient Indian civilizations, 4, 15–17, 83, 85, 89, 102–103, 140; Spanish exploration, 4, 17–19, 20, 23, 24, 54, 72; missionary activities, 20–25, 36, 54; Anglo pioneers, 40–42, 55, 58, 85, 102–103

—Politics and government: under Spanish rule, 17; under Mexican rule, 25; won by the United States, 26–28; as part of New Mexico Territory, 28; as separate territory, 32, 33, 43; effect of Civil War on, 32; capital cities, 49, 50, 90, 101; first woman in Congress, 52; struggle for statehood, 59–62, 75, 130; statehood achieved, 62, 70; constitutional convention, 66–67; Reclamation Act, 76, 90, 91; laws to help industry, 95; Republicans in power, 97–98, 119; archaic water laws, 141

—Development and growth: trapping, 25, 26, 28, 29; mining, 33, 40, 42, 50–51, 53, 61, 92; ranching, 54, 55–56, 57, 92; lumbering, 57; effect of railroads on, 36, 56–57, 60, 61; labor disputes, 68; effect of irrigation on, 85; effect of Depression on, 92–94; effect of World War II on, 94, 95, 96; of industry, 50–54, 92, 94–95, 96, 113

—Education: public school system established, 50, 105; campus at Tempe, 95–96; university at Tucson, 111–114; William R. Mathews's work for, 115; attitude toward, 116; Richard A. Harvill's contributions to, 116–117. *See also* Arizona State University; University of Arizona

—Fine arts: Arizona in literature, 6, 7–8, 15, 16, 36; Browne's description, 44–47; stage plays and stories, 56; Gila described, 79, 139; need for writers and historians, 99–100, 123; writers, 37, 124–129; artists, 124, 128, 132–135, 136; poets, 130; photographers, 136–137

Arizona Daily Star, 114, 115

Arizona Highways, 7, 124, 136–137

Arizona Historical Society: Poston's estab-

149